God's
Zeal

God's Zeal

The Battle of the Three Monotheisms

PETER SLOTERDIJK

Translated by
WIELAND HOBAN

polity

First published in German as *Gottes Eifer. Vom Kampf der drei Monotheismen* © Suhrkamp Verlag Frankfurt am Main 2007

This English edition © Polity Press, 2009

Polity Press
65 Bridge Street
Cambridge CB2 1UR, UK

Polity Press
350 Main Street
Malden, MA 02148, USA

All rights reserved. Except for the quotation of short passages for the purpose of criticism and review, no part of this publication may be reproduced, stored in a retrieval system, or transmitted, in any form or by any means, electronic, mechanical, photocopying, recording or otherwise, without the prior permission of the publisher.

ISBN-13: 978-0-7456-4506-3
ISBN-13: 978-0-7456-4507-0 (paperback)

A catalogue record for this book is available from the British Library.

Typeset in 11 on 13 pt Berling
by SNP Best-set Typesetter Ltd., Hong Kong
Printed and bound in Great Britain
by MPG Books Ltd, Bodmin, Cornwall

The publisher has used its best endeavours to ensure that the URLs for external websites referred to in this book are correct and active at the time of going to press. However, the publisher has no responsibility for the websites and can make no guarantee that a site will remain live or that the content is or will remain appropriate.

Every effort has been made to trace all copyright holders, but if any have been inadvertently overlooked the publishers will be pleased to include any necessary credits in any subsequent reprint or edition.

For further information on Polity, visit our website:
www.politybooks.com.

The translation of this work was supported by a grant from the Goethe-Institut which is funded by the German Ministry of Foreign Affairs.

Contents

	Dedication	*page* vii
1	The premises	1
2	The formations	19
3	The battle fronts	40
4	The campaigns	50
5	The matrix	82
6	The pharmaka	105
7	The parables of the ring	122
8	After-zeal	150
	Index	161

Dedication

This book is dedicated to Bazon Brock – for several reasons. Firstly because, thanks to his reflections on a normative concept of civilization, he provided one of the polar reference points for the thoughts presented here. Secondly, because his seventieth birthday, despite having taken place some months ago, offered an occasion of almost challenging quality. Finally, it was he who provoked the present study through his own personal initiative. The following text is based on a lecture I was asked to give by Bazon Brock and Yael Katz Ben Shalom on the occasion of the opening of the Artneuland gallery in Berlin on 28 November 2006, a venue that thematicizes, among other things, the development of the trialogue between the monotheistic religions in the medium of the arts – but also supports the secular exchange between Israelis, Arabs and Europeans. The mixed response to my roughly sketched, rushed oral presentation gave me something of an idea of the difficulties involved in such a project. That experience formed one of the motivations for the slightly slower, more complete exposition of my thoughts I have attempted here.

There is a further reason for my decision to dedicate this text to Bazon Brock. In the summer of 2006, on the occasion of the aforementioned birthday, I had the honour of being invited by Chris Derkon, with the patronage of

DEDICATION

Hubert Burda, to give a eulogy in the Haus der Kunst in Munich for the artist, art critic, civilization theorist, pedagogue of provocation and performance philosopher Brock. In my speech, I attempted to hold a mirror up to him in order to characterize him through similarities and contrasts with four figures from recent art and cultural history: Marcel Duchamps, Salvador Dalí, Joseph Beuys and Friedrich Nietzsche. I took the latter's concept of intellectual honesty in order to ascribe it to the jubilarian in a highly personal sense. In that context, which invited thinking in superlatives, I could take the liberty of making the following statement: 'My dear Bazon Brock, you will have to put up with my saying that you are the most honest person of our time.' On that occasion, I spoke those words in front of an audience that was at the same time a circle of friends. Now I would like to repeat them to a readership that constitutes no more or less than a public.

1

The premises

When studying the writings of philosophical authors that demand a thorough inspection of one's own discourse, one occasionally stumbles upon paragraphs that are conspicuous because they are obviously not necessitated by the course of a particular idea, but rather stem from a sudden associative urge that interrupts the development of an argument. In Hegel's *Lectures on Aesthetics*, for example, in the section dealing with the Dutch painters of the seventeenth century, the author includes that now famous reference to 'life's Sundays' – meaning those exceptional states of existence relished with such demonstrative sensual enjoyment by the people he depicts. Obviously it is not Hegel the dialectician speaking here, the thinker who knows most of what he knows systematically, rather than simply having 'picked it up' somewhere. In this passage, he is bypassing his logical apparatus and speaking as a descendant of Swabian Protestantism encountering a welcome echo of his youthful impressions in the relaxed indecency of Dutch everyday life. So even if these boisterous philistines from the damp North are anything but saints, they surely cannot be entirely bad people with such good cheer – and, when the occasion arises, he will tell the reader this in the manner of a declaration of faith. If one so desired, one could see a hidden doctrine in Hegel's formulation: as highly as we cherish what is wonderful, it is the duty of art to let the commonplace have the last word. Does the value of that trivial Sunday feeling not increase to the same degree that we grow tired of the cult of exceptional states, these continuations of the wonderful by the most extreme means?

To take a much darker example – and at the same time a much more current one – of a digression that breaks the boundaries of its context in the work of an otherwise highly controlled, even obsessively careful, author, I shall introduce a few lines from a lecture given by Jacques Derrida in spring 1993 in Riverside, California; the extended version was published as a book that same year in Paris under the title *Spectres de Marx*.[1] There, in a passage that has become notorious since, Derrida gets carried away for a moment and makes the following comment: 'The war over the "appropriation of Jerusalem" is today's world war. It is taking place everywhere, it is the world, it is the singular figure of its "out of joint"-ness today.' This eruptive statement can only be understood with reference to two pieces of information concerning Derrida and his context. Firstly, one needs to know that, in order to explore the possibility of the inextinguishable significance of Karl Marx for the post-Communist era, he had embarked on a meditation upon Hamlet's comment 'the world is out of joint' that runs through his overlong deliberations as a leitmotif. Secondly, he engaged polemically with Francis Fukuyama's theory of the 'end of history' (first put forward in 1989, then expanded into the book *The End of History and the Last Man* in 1992), in which he sees (mistakenly, I would argue) a form of liberal-technocratic evangelism and a somewhat rash, perhaps even irresponsible, version of American triumphalist rhetoric. This marks the start of a torrent of ideas culminating in the passage quoted above.

---

[1] Jacques Derrida, *Spectres of Marx* (London and New York: Routledge, 1994).

I shall place that statement by Derrida, who left us in 2004, at the head of the following reflections – not as a motto, but rather as a warning sign pointing out a particularly explosive semantic and political danger zone in today's world: the Near and Middle East, where, if Derrida was right, three messianic eschatologies embroiled in rivalry are 'directly or indirectly' mobilizing 'all the powers in the world and the entire "world order" for the ruthless war they are waging against one another'.[2] I am not sure whether I would like to adopt the thesis of the war of eschatologies unreservedly, and am well aware that it is more an example of dangerous thinking than a stylistically assured philosophical explanation, whether casual or committed. Here, Derrida of all people – that author whose reputation is tied to the procedures of 'deconstruction', the meticulous dissection of metaphysical hyperbole and one-sided discourse used as a means of power – indulged in an excursus based around one of the most pathos-ridden exaggerations ever formulated by a philosopher of recent generations.

It is clear, however, and this brings us to our subject: Derrida is here referring, directly and indirectly, to Judaism, Christianity and Islam. He is concerned with identifying the group of monotheistic religions as 'conflict parties' entangled with one another in world-historical terms. His synopsis anticipates the meanwhile popular theory of a 'clash of monotheisms', though one cannot accuse him of wanting to confront the three religious complexes with one another in their dogmatic and social totalities. He refers primarily to their missionary aspects, which are sometimes also known as their 'universalist potential', and hence those elements in each of the individual belief structures that one could describe as its 'radioactive material', its manic-activist or messianic-expansionist mass. It is with these dangerous

---

[2] Ibid.

substances that we shall concern ourselves especially in the following.[3]

My intention in placing a quotation of this kind at the start is to make it clear that none of what will be said here can, whether theologically, politically or religion-psychologically, be thought of as harmless. The following deliberations could be compared to open heart surgery – and will only be chosen by those who have reason to prevent their convictions from suffering a metaphorical heart attack. I would therefore consider it advisable to agree on some form of safety procedure with the readers before we begin. This will take the form of an arrangement as to which aspects of religion and religious faith can and must be discussed with the help of scientifically founded distortions – and which aspects most likely can or should not. I would suggest a sort of blasphemy clause, and invite the reader to decide, after taking some time for reflection, whether he or she wishes to continue reading. According to this agreement, a number of phenomena traditionally assigned to the realm of the transcendent or holy would be released for non-religious reinterpretation (of potentially blasphemous appearance, albeit not intended as such). Other areas of sacred speech and religious sentiment, however, will remain untouched for material, formal and moral reasons.

I shall address – provisionally, and without systematic intentions – seven aspects of the phenomenon of transcendence. The first four of these, as will be demonstrated shortly, are capable of being critically translated into worldly and functional categories without their religious side risking the loss of more than is always lost through the acquisition of better knowledge. I will distinguish between four incorrect interpretations of the fact of tran-

---

[3] Derrida repeats his arguments regarding the war of the monotheistic religions in a conversation with Lieven De Cauter from 19 February 2004 entitled 'Pour une justice à venir', in which he sketches the outlines of a formalized or non-religious messianism.

scendence and two further aspects that I would not wish to present as entirely immune to misunderstanding, but which, owing to their objectively mysterious character, offer resistance to any simplistic projection onto natural and social contexts. I will then address a seventh, highly sensitive aspect, showing that its undecidable nature places it beyond the difference between knowledge and faith – though it is faith, conspicuously enough, that profits most often from this state of affairs.

Let us begin with a thesis presented not long ago by Heiner Mühlmann, in a recent essay on cultures as learning units, in the form of a resolute question followed by a succinct answer: 'How does transcendence come about? It comes about through the misunderstanding of slowness.' The author clarifies: 'A movement is slow if it takes longer than a generation. In order to observe it, we must depend on co-operation with those who lived before us and those who will live after us.'[4] As co-operations with previous and subsequent generations have been either only rarely achieved or structurally impossible, and at best remained precarious episodes, it is understandable that, in previous times, most of these slow phenomena were consigned to the realm of transcendence, which here means: to the realm of the unobservable. As a result, they could be declared subject to the otherworldly plans of some transhuman or divine intelligence, and no objection would have had any chance of success. As soon as

---

[4] Heiner Mühlmann, 'Die Ökonomiemaschine' [The Economy Machine], in 5 Codes. Architektur, Paranoia und Risiko in Zeiten des Terrors [Architecture, Paranoia and Risk in Times of Terror], ed. Gerd de Bruyn and Igmade (Basle, Boston and Berlin, 2006), p. 227. One could possibly make this thesis more specific by replacing the word 'generation' with the phrase 'learning phase of an average individual life-span' – this would, in the retrospective dimension, demand a co-operation with the knowledge of ancestors one did not have the chance to know (this normally means one's great-grandparents and earlier), and prospectively also a co-operation with the descendants one will not live to know (starting with one's great-grandchildren).

technologically and scientifically matured civilizations develop effective methods for the observation of slow phenomena, however, the concept of transcendental planning loses a considerable part of its plausibility – whether it is known as creation, prediction, predestination, salvation history or the like – and makes room for immanent procedures serving the interpretation of long-term processes. These means can encompass biological or sociosystemic evolution theories, wave models and crack theories that allow a description of oscillations and mutations in the realm of the *longue durée*. Only then can the difficulties and failures of evolution be assessed in their full extent, without the forced positivism of the creation idea compelling us to look away. In orthodox communities where identification with the edifying notion of transcendental planning is still very intense, one can observe militant resistance to the conceptual means leading to the secularization of those slow phenomena previously consigned to the hereafter. This is exemplified most clearly by the creationists in the USA, who are known to resort to all manner of methods in order to immunize their doctrine of sudden, intentional creation against the new sciences of slow, self-organized becoming.[5]

The second step lies in recognizing the following: transcendence also arises from the misunderstanding of vehemence. In order to clarify this idea, I shall draw once again on a concept introduced into the cultural sciences by Heiner Mühlmann – namely the link between stress analysis and the theory of the determinate formation of rituals and symbols laid out in his epochal programmatic text *The Nature of Cultures*. This work – encouraged by sug-

---

[5] We are indebted to the creationists for the amazing idea that God created the world around 4000 BC in such a way that it appears immeasurably older than it actually is (theorem of the illusion of age). The spiritual price of the response to the evolutionist challenge is high: it turns God into a *genius malignus* who, even during the creation itself, did not leave out any opportunity to set the evolutionists on the wrong track one day.

gestions from Bazon Brock – introduced a radically new paradigm for the combining of cultural science and evolution theory into the debate.[6] The phenomenology of the great stress reaction in *homo sapiens* and the ways in which cultures have sought to cope with it make it clear why, to the subject of stress, the conditions experienced often seem be of a transcendent nature. The vehemence of endogenous processes – which are initially strictly biologically determined, though very often cloaked by symbolism – can, in some cases, reach such a level that what is experienced is inevitably attributed to external forces.

Within our space of tradition, the model for this is provided by the wrath of Achilles as recounted by Homer, invoked throughout millennia by the warriors of the old Europe as the numinous origin of their noble and cruel profession. Undoubtedly heroic wrath is part of the same phenomenon as the manifestations of battle frenzy found in numerous cultures, which can in turn be compared to prophetic ecstasies. In physiological terms, the episodes of heroic fury show the result of an identification of the warrior with the propulsive energies that overcome him. It belongs within the spectrum of berserker enthusiasms, which includes the well-known amok syndrome of the Malaysian peoples (eagerly taken up by Western mass culture and pop-psychologically instrumentalized from within as an example of the wild), alongside the ecstatic rapture of the Vedic warriors or the battle rage of the Germanic heroes, which extended even to a lust for their own demise. In almost every case this fury, in the eyes of its bearers, seems to take, almost by necessity, the form of an obsession inspired from above, in which the martial energy of the agent is completely absorbed, making the battle appear to him as a mission. As a primal form of endogenous revelatory experience, fury constitutes

---

[6] Heiner Mühlmann, *Die Natur der Kulturen. Entwurf einer kulturgenetischen Theorie* [The Nature of Cultures: Outline of a Culture-Genetic Theory] (Vienna and New York, 1996).

something like the natural religion of the impassioned. As long as the transcendental misunderstanding of vehemence predominates, it is impossible to see how something that is experienced as an inspiration of strength could arise from a psychosemantically influenced process initiated from within the organism when it is subjected to extreme stress – a description that would presumably also apply to a considerable number of prophetic ecstasies.

Furthermore, this massive reaction to stress manifests itself in not only an explosive, but also an implosive, mode. There was an example of this a number of years ago, at a bullfight in one of the most important arenas in Madrid. The matador had made three failed attempts to deal the deadly blow to the charging bull – upon which he was seized by a sort of dumbfounded numbness, a state in which he would have been run down or killed by the raging animal if his colleagues had not carried the paralysed bullfighter from the arena. The scene can best be understood by recognizing in it the reversal of the stress reaction into an ecstasy of self-rejection. In that moment, shame revealed itself to the failed matador (in Spanish: *the killer*) like some otherworldly force. Although the physiological side of the incident is thus not especially mysterious, its spiritual aspect is at least somewhat harder to pin down. But we can certainly speculate: if one established a connection to the religious sphere, this should remind us to what extent the God who judges humanity also has the power of damnation. Whoever finds themselves wishing the ground would swallow them up not only feels the disadvantage of being visible, but also has an immediate understanding of what it means for one's own name to be erased from the Book of Life. This much is clear: the connection between guilt, shame and stress, without which the fervour of some religious subjects against themselves would be inconceivable, is rooted in endogenous mechanisms that are open to psychobiological elucidation. Much of what Rudolf Otto refers to in his well-known book *Das Heilige* as the *mysterium tremendum*[7] lies *de jure* within the realm of stress theory. Taken as a whole, Otto's study – despite certain achievements towards a clarification of the objective field – can be considered a solemn misunderstanding of vehemence. In the *fear and trembling* side of religion often cited since Otto, one finds a manifestation of the neurosemantically significant fact that artificially induced extremes of experience appear at the ritual centre of all those religions which have succeeded in maintaining a lasting tradition. Paradoxically, it has been precisely the monotheistic scriptural religions, apparently endangered by the paleness of the letter, that have shown a great aptitude in finding a solid foundation in effective ritualizations of the most extreme arousal. Only in this way have they been able to secure their inscription on the involuntary memories of the faithful.

A third form of transcendence that is open to elucidation stems from a misunderstanding of what I call the 'inaccessibility of the other'. I shall briefly illustrate what this means with an example from a classic work of modern literature. Towards the end of the second part of his novel tetralogy *Joseph and his Brothers*, written in 1934, Thomas Mann describes how Jacob, having received the news of his favourite son Joseph's alleged death, embarks on an excessive ritual of mourning: he perches himself on a rubbish heap in his courtyard, as Job later did, and hurls laments, accusations and protests at God and fate over endless days and weeks. Once the first wave of grief has subsided, Jacob realizes how improperly he has behaved – and now begins to see it as a great advantage that God did not react like some offended spouse or partner to

---

[7] Rudolf Otto, *Das Heilige. Über das Irrationale in der Idee des Göttlichen und sein Verhältnis zum Rationalen* [The Holy: On the Irrational in the Idea of the Divine and Its Connection to the Rational] (Munich, 1917/1987), pp. 13–28.

everything he said in his heated state, rather choosing to conceal himself through remoteness; Thomas Mann speaks subtly of Jacob's provocative 'impetuous misery' [*Elendsübermut*], which God fortunately ignored 'with silent tolerance'. Clearly one should first of all interpret God's calm non-reaction, which some theologians make quite some fuss about, in a more plausible fashion, both here and elsewhere. It is initially no more than a simple case of inaccessibility, and a number of substantial conditions would have to be met before one could conclude that someone who does not react is therefore a superior, indeed transcendent, other. If one were to tell a deaf-mute the story of one's life, one should not conclude from his silence that he prefers to keep his comments to himself. In such situations, transcendence arises from an over-interpretation of unresponsiveness. It results from the fact that some others are initially – and largely – unreachable, and therefore remain independent from us. Hence they lie outside of the fantasies of symmetry that determine our usual notions of reply, understanding, retaliation and the like. This discovery can lead to the formation of sensible relationships between people, relationships characterized by the hygiene of proper distance. The independence of the other is the stumbling block for any delusional search for partnership – this failure, however, constitutes a great step on the way to a freedom capable of relationships. The appropriate response to an encounter with an intelligence that remains free even in the act of co-operation is therefore gratitude for the independence of the other. So even if we are dealing here with a conception of transcendence marked by misjudgement, one should honour 'God' – in so far as this means the ultimate other – as a morally fruitful concept that attunes humans to dealing with an unmanipulable communicative counterpart.

Finally, the development of an important part of immanently transferable transcendence can be traced back to an overlooking of immune functions. Immune systems are the embodiments of expectations of injury. At the biological level they manifest themselves in the ability to form antibodies, at the legal level in the form of procedures to compensate for injustice and aggression, at the magical level in the form of protective spells, at the religious level in the shape of rituals to overcome chaos – the latter show people how to carry on when, by human reckoning, there is no way forward. From a systemic point of view – and perceived through the prism of functional distortions – religions can be defined as psychosemantic institutions with a dual focus. On the one hand, they specialize in dealing with impairments of integrity and devote themselves, thus viewed, to a wide range of psycho- and sociotherapeutic causes. On the other hand, they serve to channel and encode the human talent for excess – a function that, since European Romanticism, has largely been handed over to the art system.

At the centre of the first functional circle lies the need to give meaning to suffering, death, disorder and chance. This service, which combines the consolation of individuals with the ritual consolidation of groups, is often granted at the price of an unpredictable side effect: the edifying effects of religions are inevitably tied to ritualized speech acts, and thus attached to the level of symbolic generalization. Something that should function as a cure must simultaneously present itself as a symbolically structured conception of the world, i.e. as an ensemble of truths with claims to practical and theoretical validity. This contains the seed of a confusion of categories with virtually explosive consequences. It is the same as the temptation to elevate a pharmakon to the level of a deity. Because several symbolically stabilized immune systems normally exist alongside one another, all circulating their generalizations simultaneously, it is inevitable that these will question – or even, depending on the intensity of their respective claims to generality, partially or totally negate – one another. When there are collisions between such systems, the task of instilling edifying thoughts – or more generally, of imposing order on life by placing a frame around it – is combined with the need to be right. In order to do justice to conflicts of this type, one would have to imagine Prozac patients and Valium users accusing each other of heresy and warning of grave loss of health if the other does not convert to using the same medication. I have chosen the names of sedatives that, as we know, occasionally fail to achieve the desired effect and trigger manic states instead. The phenomenon known since St Paul's day as 'faith' has always been accompanied by a comparable risk. The welcome psychosemantic effects of religious conviction, namely the spiritual stabilization and social integration of believers, are tied to dangerous effects that correspond closely with the aforementioned manic reaction – since long before the beginning of monotheistic religions, one should add. One should therefore not take the well-documented fact that the formulation of the expansive monotheisms arose from their founders' states of manic-apocalyptic arousal lightly. The overlooking of the immune function here has a direct effect on the notion of truth. Whereas the pragmatic mentality contents itself with the belief that whatever helps is true, zealous behaviour insists on the axiom that truth is only to be found in a belief system which is entitled to demand universal subordination. Here the danger comes from the zealous tendency of a misunderstood claim to theoretical validity.

The arguments mentioned thus far follow, of course, the tradition of David Hume's work *The Natural History of Religion* from 1757, though – unlike the early Enlightenment – they no longer reduce religious ideas merely to primitive 'hopes and fears'. Certainly wishful thinking and affects of avoidance are still important factors, but they do not fully explain the religious phenomenon. The renovated version of the criticism of religion follows on from certain concepts in general cultural theory, which asks under what conditions cultural programmes achieve horizontal coherence, vertical capacity for continuation and personal internalization within a given populace.

Thanks to its complex view, the new approach also permits detailed insights into the natural and social history of false conclusions. In contrast to the classics of the Enlightenment, the new descriptions of religious aspects sketched here do not explain certain manifestations of faith through natural human error; rather, they see them as surplus phenomena that chronically expose humans to an excess of uplifting and unifying energies. The updated natural history of religion falls back on an anthropology of overreaction; this permits an illumination of the evolution of *Homo sapiens* through a theory of luxuriating surplus drives within insulated groups.[8] These surpluses would include those of consciousness that make human existence effusive or enigmatic. The concepts of surplus and overreaction do not only help to understand the energetic side of religious phenomena – they also shed light on the actual tenets of faith, as every single theopoesis is based on the universals of exaggeration.

I shall also mention a fifth aspect of transcendence for which, in my opinion, there are no functionalist or naturalist substitute descriptions of a binding nature that can be brought into the debate. Some philosophical and religious authors have articulated the thought that one element of human intelligence is the ability to imagine another intelligence superior to itself. This uplift, even if it often takes place as a mere formality, carries intelligence

---

[8] See Peter Sloterdijk, *Sphären II, Globen, Makrosphärologie* [Spheres II: Globes, Macrospherology] (Frankfurt am Main: Suhrkamp, 1999), ch. 2, 'Gefäß-Erinnerungen. Über den Grund der Solidarität in der inklusiven Form' [Container Memories: On the Reason for Solidarity in the Inclusive Form], pp. 197–250, and ch. 3, 'Archen, Stadtmauern, Weltgrenzen, Immunsysteme. Zur Ontologie des ummauerten Raums' [Arks, City Walls, World Borders, Immune Systems: On the Ontology of the Walled Space], pp. 251–325; also *Sphären III, Schäume, Plurale Sphärologie* [Spheres III: Foams, Plural Spherology] (Frankfurt am Main: Suhrkamp, 2004), ch. 3, 'Auftrieb und Verwöhnung. Zur Kritik der reinen Laune' [Impetus and Spoiling: On the Critique of Pure Mood], pp. 671f.

beyond its normal level. It shows it that understanding itself properly depends on recognizing the vertical tension to which it is subject. It is in this tension that it can grow – assuming it chooses the risk entailed by learning. Intelligence always lives within its internal surplus or deficit, and through the gesture of taking the higher pole as its model, intelligence declares its own peculiar form of transcendence. There is no need for us to concern ourselves with the variety of such gestures in the monotheistic religions (typically expressed as an insistence on studying the scriptures) and in classical philosophy (which equates suffering with learning) in the present context – it lives on in the world of books as the piety of eager readers.

Taking into account people's responses to the provocation of thinking through the inevitability of death brings us into contact with a further irreducible aspect of religious behaviour. It is above all the topological aspect of the death question that opens the door to transcendence in an entirely different sense. Mortals – to use the Greek title for humans – have always been under pressure to imagine the place the departed have 'gone to', and to which they too will 'migrate' *post mortem*. It is undeniable that this subject stimulates the imagination to bring forth remarkable fruits, as is particularly evident from the detailed depictions of places in the hereafter, of both paradisaic and infernal varieties – but the problem here goes far beyond a diagnostic observation of projective fantasies. One cannot create a simple continuum between the spatial and locative understanding of the living and their imaginary ideas of 'places' in the beyond. Therefore, the place of the dead remains transcendent in a sense of the word that requires clarification. It constitutes a heterotopic standard – if it expresses the belief that the dead are 'dwelling' in an elsewhere that eludes the alternatives of somewhere and nowhere. Tradition offers highly divergent encodings for this 'xenolocative' elsewhere, ranging from the phrase 'with God' to 'in Nirvana' or 'in the memory of those who love'. As illustrative, ambiguous and vague as these characterizations may be, their obstinate peculiarity resists any hasty reductions to a trivial nowhere.

Finally, I would like to mention a seventh meaning of transcendence that likewise cannot easily be disposed of in favour of a simple naturalistic explanation. It is coupled with the belief that a higher power beyond, usually known as 'God', turns its attention to individual humans in special moments – out of love, sympathy or outrage – and chooses them as recipients of messages that, following certain criteria of authentication, are interpreted as revelations. This is not the place to discuss the implications of the concept of revelation.[9] The expression only takes on meaning in a mode of thinking – based on many presuppositions – that I have referred to elsewhere as the 'metaphysics of the strong sender'.[10] In this context, transcendence indicates the provenance of a message of life-altering significance to humans. The idea of revelation implies a rather dramatic scenario in which a ruler who is willing to communicate addresses himself to a group of recipients through dictates that are presents, or presents that are dictates, using selected media – prophets, lawmakers and holy superhumans – in order to convince them to accept his message. At a first reading, then, revelation means a message 'from beyond' that obliges its recipient to submit gratefully.

Viewed from this perspective, the concept of revelation unmistakably belongs to the world of *Homo hierarchicus*. It sets up an analogy between the feudal relationship of lord and vassal and the cognitive relationship of object and

---

[9] See pp. 17 and 141 below.
[10] See Sloterdijk, *Sphären II*, ch. 7, 'Wie durch das reine Medium die Sphärenmitte in die Ferne wirkt. Zur Metaphysik der Telekommunikation' [How the Centre of the Sphere Affects Things Distant Through the Pure Medium: On the Metaphysics of Telecommunication], pp. 667–787.

subject, with a clear emphasis on the primacy of the lord and the object. According to this model, the receipt of a revelation corresponds to the extreme of vassalic passivity. It marks a case in which listening and obeying coincide; in other contexts one would speak of an offer that cannot be refused. It is immediately clear why this model loses its plausibility, both socially and epistemologically, in cultures characterized by devassalization. The notion of purely receptive subjects transpires as logically and empirically untenable. The subject could not reply to the angel of the object: 'May it be as you have said'; on the contrary, it knows that it impresses its own 'frame of possibilities' upon all the objects it experiences. For this and other reasons, the idea of a revelation that can be dictated and passively accepted reaches a point of crisis. Whatever is made known to subjects, and whoever does so, it can no longer be conceived of without the contribution of its recipient. It remains to be seen whether, as some constructivists claim, this extends to the point of a primacy of the receptive side.

The 'turn towards the subject' not only makes revelation depassivize itself – it also enables it to free itself increasingly from narrower religious contexts: it can no longer be restricted exclusively to the unique declaration of a transcendent sender, as in the case of a holy scripture – it now takes place at all times and in all places, firstly due to the openness of the world that 'clears'[11] itself, and secondly due to the forced disclosure of something previously concealed that is advanced by enlightenment and organized research. The facts of the science industry and artistic creation in modern times offer unambiguous proof that the era of merely received revelations has come to an end. The activist culture of rationality has seen the development of a strong antithesis to the passivism of ancient

---

[11] Translator's note: the use of *lichten* in the original refers to Heidegger's existential notion of a clearing (*Lichtung*), i.e. to clear in the sense of opening or illumination rather than ordering.

and mediaeval times that is waiting to be understood by the advocates of the older concept of revelation. The devotees of the old ways are faced with the task of acknowledging how gravely they have overestimated religious revelation as the key to the nature of all things, and underestimated the illumination of the world through awareness in life, science and art. This places theology under pressure to learn, as it must not allow the connection with the worldly knowledge of the other side to be broken. Without a certain convergence of the tenets of religious revelation and non-religious worldly illumination, the thoughts of the religious would be taken over by irrational arbitrariness. This is of direct relevance to the idea of 'faith', as the active aspect grows not only in comparison to the passive, but also relative to it, through progressive modernization – until it finally becomes clear how strongly the 'will to faith' asserts primacy over the gift of belief.[12]

Space does not permit a development of the point that the permeation of religion through activist motives leads to a reformation – or likewise of the observation that the intellectual-historical figure of 'counter-reformation' comes into play whenever there is an attempt to re-enforce passivity. In this sense, a large portion of current mass culture, especially its horrendous side, can be considered part of an undeclared counter-reformation: this is what has paved the way for the much-vaunted 'return of religion'. All projects aimed at a restoration of passivity show the will to faith acting as a longing to be overpowered. In this context it would be apposite to address Martin Mosebach's striking statement that we believe with our knees – 'or we do not believe at all':[13] it is symptomatic

---

[12] See Peter Sloterdijk, 'Neuigkeiten über den Willen zum Glauben. Notiz über Desäkularisation' [News of the Will to Faith: A Note on Desecularization], Bochum, 10 February 2007.

[13] Martin Mosebach, *Häresie der Formlosigkeit. Die römische Liturgie und ihr Feind* [The Heresy of Formlessness: The Roman Liturgy and its Enemy], new extended edition (Munich, 2007), p. 25.

of a determined quest to find a foothold in the objective realm. If it is true, the knees would be the true Catholic organs and the uplifted hearts would have to content themselves with second place.

To summarize, I would posit that the study of such phenomena will no longer be restricted to the religious sciences in future. Rather, the field of general cultural science must ultimately expand its jurisdiction to encompass the realm of religion; instead of a year of the humanities,[14] one should declare a century of cultural science. Its spiritual mission should become clear as soon as it learns to convert the treasures of transcultural knowledge into live forms of capital that can be invested in all existing cultures. As a science of coexistence, cultural science would be the true moderator of global ecumenism. *It* has the responsibility of showing why the path of civilization is the only one that is still open.

---

[14] Translator's note: the German Ministry of Education declared 2007 'das Jahr der Geisteswissenschaften'.

2

The formations

Having laid out these conditions, I would like to turn my attention to the trio of monotheistic religions, whose war and dialogue form the object of these reflections. I shall begin with a genetic observation intended to show how those religions developed in sequence from one another, or from older sources – in a manner comparable to a three-phase explosion (or a series of enemy takeovers). The fact that such a rapid sketch inevitably contains only elementary and highly schematicized observations does not require an explanation of its own, and as we are not dealing with a history of religion, but rather a presentation of 'conflict parties', I can restrict myself to descriptions of a typological nature. Nor will I be focusing on the history of the holy texts, which is why there is not the slightest attempt here to relate the unfolding of Christianity and Islam as the adventure novel of misreading that literary critics recognize in the approach of the two later monotheisms to the holy books of their predecessors.[1] There is no need to emphasize that, from the perspective of faith, the following reflections will no doubt seem grossly unjust in many places – in so far as most things said about faith

---

[1] Regarding the Christian misreading of Jewish sources, especially in the cases of Paul's epistles and the gospel of John, see Harold Bloom, *Jesus and Jahweh. The Names Divine* (New York, 2005).

without allowing it a chance to revise them are unjust. A fitful shaking of heads by all three parties as a readers' commentary on the thoughts that follow can scarcely be avoided. One should bear in mind that the topic as such encourages one-sidedness, as it demands a foregrounding not of the awe-inspiring foundations of the monotheistic teachings, but rather of their potential for competition and conflict.

It is only logical to begin the nomination of candidates in the monotheistic field of theses by determining the position of Judaism. The question that will concern us here was given its quintessential expression by Thomas Mann in an inspired chapter of *Joseph and his Brothers* under the heading 'How Abraham discovered God'. In the literarily reconstructed primal scene of the Abrahamic tradition, we observe the forefather of monotheism struggling with the question of whom humanity should serve: '. . . and his strange answer had been: "The highest alone"'.[2] In a strenuous meditation, Abraham reaches the conclusion that Mother Earth, as admirably diverse as her fruits may be, surely cannot be the first and highest authority, as she is obviously dependent on the rain that falls from the sky. Led to the sky by his thoughts, he concludes after a while that, in spite of its sublime constellations and all the terrifying meteorological phenomena, it too cannot quite embody what he is looking for, as those phenomena constantly change and negate one another – the moonlight, for example, fades when the morning star rises. 'No, they too are not worthy to be my gods.' Finally, through his sheer 'urge for the highest',[3] Abraham arrives at the concept of an absolutely sublime, powerful and otherworldly God who rules over the stars

---

[2] Thomas Mann, *Joseph und seine Brüder, Die Geschichten Jacobs. Der junge Joseph* (Frankfurt am Main: Fischer, 1983), p. 316. English edition: *Joseph and his Brothers*, trans. John E. Woods (New York: Everyman's Library, 2005).
[3] Mann, *Joseph und seine Brüder*, p. 317.

and thus transpires as the foremost, mightiest, only god. From this point on, Abraham, having himself become the 'father of God',[4] so to speak, through his investigations, knew to whom all should now rightfully pray: 'There had only ever been He, the most high, who alone could be the rightful God of men and the one and only object of their cries for help and songs of praise.'[5]

In his poetic exploration of the psychodynamic source of monotheistic belief in the soul of the progenitor of the Jewish people, Thomas Mann placed a highly fitting emphasis on an impulse that has been referred to as the summotheistic affect. Long before there was such a thing as theoretical theology, it was this feeling that provided the template for authentic monotheistic belief. It creates a resonance between a God who is serious about his dominion over the earth and a human who is serious about his desire to belong to such a sovereign deity. Thomas Mann does not omit to mention that a quest for God of this kind is inseparable from the striving for human significance: so there can be no monotheism without a certain self-importance. 'In order to make some kind of impression and achieve a certain significance before God and men, it was necessary to take things – or at least one thing – very seriously. Father Abraham had taken the question of whom man should serve absolutely seriously . . .'[6]

Strangely enough, Abraham's momentous elevation of God (as shown by his portrait in the books of the Yahwist) did not immediately remove him to a completely superhuman realm. Certainly he is described as a god above, but there is no doubt that he is in touch with earthly reality. He retains all the attributes of a human who is no stranger to anything all too human, ranging from the wild temper he displays in his dealings with his subjects to the

---

[4] Ibid., p. 319.
[5] Ibid., p. 318.
[6] Ibid., p. 316.

unpredictable explosiveness of his early utterances. His despotic irony and constant fluctuation between presence and absence make him appear more like an insufferable father than a principle of divine justice. A god who loves gardens and basks in their cool evening air, who fights bloody battles and imposes sadistic tests of subordination on his believers, could be almost anything – but not a discarnate spirit, let alone some neuter otherworldly being. His affective life vacillates between joviality and tumult, and nothing could be more absurd than the claim that his intention is to love the human race in its entirety. If there was ever a figure that could be said to be wholly god and wholly human, it was Yahweh as represented in the Yahwist. Harold Bloom rightly characterized him as the most untameable figure in religious history – the King Lear of the heavenly rulers, one could say. The notion that a charismatic dreamer like Jesus, of all people, could have been his 'beloved son' – even one and the same being, as the Nicene theologians claimed – is theopsychologically unthinkable.[7] No one can be *homoousios* with such a paragon of wilfulness, least of all a 'son' like Jesus. What the Christian theologians called God the Father was actually a late reinvention for trinity-political purposes; at that time it was necessary to introduce a benevolent father to match, at least to a degree, the amazing son. The Christian redescription of God naturally had very little to do with the Yahweh of Jewish scripture.

At the start of the monotheistic chain of reaction we find a form of contract between a great, serious psyche and a great, serious God. There is no need to dwell on his other qualities – his choleric temperament, his irony and his taste for thunderous hyperbole – in this context. This alliance creates a major symbol-producing relationship without which most of what have, since the nineteenth century, been termed 'advanced civilizations' (since Karl

---

[7] See Bloom, *Jesus and Jahweh*.

Jaspers, also known as 'axial age civilizations') would be inconceivable. One of the secrets of the summotheistic alliance certainly lies in the satisfaction of believers that, by submitting to the highest, they can share in some part, however modest, of his sovereignty. Hence the pronounced joy at submission that can be observed among partisans of the strict idea of God. No one can take the step towards such a God without being intoxicated by the desire to serve and belong. Quite often, resolute servants of the One are enraptured by pride at their own humility. When the faithful bloom in their zealous roles, this is partly also because nothing dispels the ghosts of existential disorientation as effectively as participation in a sacred enterprise that creates jobs and promises advancement. In this sense, the system known as 'God' can be viewed as the most important employer in the Holy Land – in which case atheism constitutes a form of employment destruction that is, understandably, fought bitterly by those affected.

The liaison of seriousness and greatness corresponds to the growing pressure to which the religious sensibility is subjected as soon as the requirements for the status of divinity increase. And their evolutionary increase is inevitable when, as in the Middle East of the first and second millennia BC, several ambitious religions begin to come into conflict with one another – until the phase of diplomatic niceties is over and the question of final priority and absolute supremacy becomes unavoidable. Under these conditions, the connections between the psyche and the world take on a new dynamic: the expanded scene of the world and God demands greater powers of comprehension among the faithful souls – and, vice versa, the increasing demands for meaning directed at God and the world by those souls call for increasingly interesting roles in the general dramas. The monotheistic zealots of all periods testify to this development with their entire existence: if they had their way, their subservient passion would not simply be their private contribution to the glory of God. It would be the zeal of God himself reaching through them and into the world. This zeal, correctly understood, is an aspect of God's regret at having created the world. In its milder form, it shows his benevolent will to salvage what he still can of a creation that has got out of control.

Abraham's choice of religion, then, is extremely *thymotically* determined – if it is indeed legitimate to bring the Greek concept denoting the activity centre of the psyche's ambition- and pride-based impulses, the *thymós*, into play in the interpretation of the Middle Eastern theodramas.[8] In demanding that his God should be the absolute highest, so high as to be above the world, Abraham ruled out – to the great advantage of his self-confidence – all lesser alliances in his search for a sovereign lord and partner. The price of this singular alliance was monolatry: honouring a single God, raised above a wealth of rivals whose existence and effect could not, for the time being, be denied. Friedrich Max Müller (1823–1900), the great linguistic and theological researcher influenced by Schelling, to whom contemporary Indology still owes a great deal today, suggested the term *henotheism* for this position devoted to the cult of the One and Only, and identified it as the evolutionary forerunner of monotheism. In so far as this One takes on the pre-eminence of the only significant one, the remaining gods are naturally relegated to the lower ranks. In time they come to be seen as no more than obsolete forces, or at most helpful celestial functionaries, but more often as rebellious parasites – points of departure for the tracts on demons and devils whose blossoming was to become so typical of the later, more developed monotheistic doctrines. One can understand, therefore, why there can never be monotheism without ranking-based jealousy. As the figure of the One and Only could be guaranteed exclusively through the

---

[8] For a reintroduction of thymotic psychology into current discourse, see Peter Sloterdijk, *Zorn und Zeit. Politisch-psychologischer Versuch* [Anger and Time. A Politico-Psychological Essay] (Frankfurt am Main: Suhrkamp, 2006).

subordination of other candidates, keeping the rejected ones under control was to remain a perennial task. The earliest monotheistic matrix already contains the outlines of the areas that would later be filled by the One and Only's adversaries on duty. This new opposition showed its polemic tendencies early on: the transcendent, true One against the inner-worldly, false many.

The aspect that lends monotheism its bold difficulty from a theoretical perspective – it's a-priori decision to imagine transcendence as a person – shows its greatest advantage on the practical side of things: that any potential or actual believer can fall back on a wealth of intuitions that make God's actions towards the world comprehensible. If God is a person, he can create, destroy, love, hate, allow, forbid, reward and punish like a person – and, while doing all those things, observe.[9] As long as one was merely dealing with household and family gods, it was easy to make this seem plausible. In order to equip a world god with such personal attributes, however, it was probably inevitable that one would at least have to refer to great kings as an analogy. Without any counter-intuitive efforts, however, nothing would be achieved in this field. One thing, at any rate, is certain: only by suggesting a personified God was early monotheism able to carry out its most ambitious manoeuvre, namely setting up something utterly improbable as the greatest certainty of faith.

Looking at the establishment of Jewish monotheism, one must also take into account two psycho-political complications of no little consequence. Firstly, a suspicion was voiced that it was based on an exported idea that the Jews had taken with them on their semi-mythological exodus from Egypt under the leadership of Moses – a suspicion that Sigmund Freud expanded into the

---

[9] See Niklas Luhmann, *Die Religion der Gesellschaft* [The Religion of Society], ed. André Kieserling (Frankfurt am Main: Suhrkamp, 2002), pp. 152f.

daredevil theory that Moses himself, as his name suggests, was an Egyptian, possibly from a noble family, who was continuing the large-scale religio-political experiment of the Amarna period, the solar monotheism of Akhenaten, among the Jews. Then the Jews of the post-Mosaic period would, in spite of their anti-Egyptian self-image, have remained a hetero-Egyptian collective[10] with which – semi-consciously at first, then unconsciously – a chapter of experimental High God theology was enacted with all its consequences – consequences of which the internal genocide carried out by the faithful followers of Moses against the worshippers of the golden calf at the foot of Mount Sinai (assuming this incident is not simply a concoction to edify and terrify) would perhaps have been an extreme, but not entirely ineffective, example.

Moses' command 'let every man kill his brother, his friend and his neighbour' (Exodus 32:27) marks the first appearance of the motto of that zeal for the One and Only that makes long stretches of the history of monotheism (specifically in its Christian and Islamic edits) read like an account of righteous ruthlessness. A new moral quality for killing was invented at Mount Sinai: it no longer served the survival of a tribe, but rather the triumph of a principle. Once God becomes an idea . . . This innovation was connected to a change in the nature of the victim that led from the offering of a gift to the extermination of an opponent. One can only speak of Israel's breakthrough to the founding of a 'voluntary community of belief' if one passes over the faction that was exterminated.[11] The

---

[10] Regarding 'hetero-Egypticism', see Peter Sloterdijk, *Derrida ein Ägypter. Vom Problem der jüdischen Pyramide* [Derrida, an Egyptian. Concerning the Problem of the Jewish Pyramid] (Polity Press, 2009).

[11] This aspect is emphasized by Gottfried Schramm in his study *Fünf Wegscheiden der Weltgeschichte* [Five Turning Points in World History] (Göttingen, 2004), pp. 28–30, in order to explain the way in which innovative groups push on towards new fundamental insights which they then follow spontaneously; this phenomenon is only

system of denunciation set up by the Jacobins after 1793 shows just what 'communities of belief' are capable of under stress: it commanded the virtuous among the French populace to report not only their closest neighbours but even their own family members to the organs of revolutionary justice for the slightest of critical remarks.

The myth of the exodus remains constitutive for Judaism as, through its dramatic circumstances that are invoked time and again, it creates a strong psychic engram – not least through the admonitory reminder of the deeds of the angel of death, who passed over the Jewish doorways that had been marked with lamb's blood (Hebrew *pessach*: leave out, pass over, spare) while entering the houses of the Egyptians and murdering their firstborn. The exodus story is unmistakably embedded within a maximum stress ritual which, because of its powerful memoactivity, guarantees the practising community the greatest possible internalization of laws.[12] Anyone looking for the secret of how Judaism was able to survive for over three millennia should begin here. It is nothing other than the high degree of memoactive fitness inherent in this religion because of its primary myth: it combines the joy at having escaped with the memory of that most terrible of nights. Numerous secondary forms of rehearsal support these first influences, especially ones centred around scriptural study. The proud painfulness of circumcision may have had a similar effect. Whoever lives under the myth of the exodus shares a stable stigma that distresses, elevates, obliges, bonds and excludes. Its eminent duplicability enables its carriers to pass on their passion and

---

genuinely evident among the early Christians, the Reformation of the sixteenth century and the American revolution of the eighteenth century, however, though one could almost cite early Mosaism as a counterexample.

[12] For information on ritually induced memoactive stress as a vehicle for the inculturation of culturally specific teachings, see Heiner Mühlmann, *Jesus überlistet Darwin* [Jesus Outwits Darwin] (Vienna and New York, 2007).

wander through the ages as living transporters of spiritual content.

The second complicating precondition of the monotheistic establishment of biblical Israel stems from its experiences in exile during the sixth century BC. There is a wide-ranging consensus among scholars that Jewish theology entered its critical phase in the time of Babylonian captivity (586–538 BC), when it developed the characteristics that can still be recognized today. Following earlier zealotic preludes and rigorist episodes, these were the years of monotheistic decision. This escalation was triggered by the semantic clinch between the God of the Israelites and the imperial Gods of Babylon. The earlier Yahweh monolatry now brought forth a speculative superstructure that developed into a monotheism that was both theoretically and politically advanced.[13] The point of these radicalizations is not difficult to identify. It lies in the emergence of a political concept of God with metapolitical overtones that testifies to the resolve to grant the God of the enslaved people – weeping at the waters of Babylon – absolute superiority, albeit one concealed and for the meantime only capable of being asserted symbolically, over the gods of the despotic empire.

This turning point constitutes one of the most significant moments in the intellectual history of the later West. It marks the first separation of spirit and power, previously a diffuse unity, into polar opposites. While the rulers in power, like all happy tyrants before them, paid unwavering tribute to worldly success and accumulated reports of victories like holy trophies, the spirit of the defeated

---

[13] Matthias Albani, *Der eine Gott und die himmlischen Heerscharen. Zur Begründung des Monotheismus bei Deuterojesaja im Horizont der Astralisierung des Gottesverständnisses im Alten Orient* [The One God and the Heavenly Host. The Foundation of Monotheism in Deutero-Isaiah in the Horizon of the Astralization of the Concept of God in the Ancient Orient] (Leipzig, 2000); also André Lemaire, *Naissance du monothéisme. Point de vue d'un historien* [The Birth of Monotheism. A Historian's Point of View] (Paris, 2003).

withdrew to a sanctuary in which it dreamt of justice and dictated the conditions for its imminent satisfaction. In this context, the concept of truth took on a futuristic tinge and opened itself up for reversal fantasies of a partly therapeutic, partly retributionist nature. Post-Babylonian theology discovered the counterfactual and utopian mode of thinking. Truth and reality parted ways, presenting the option of propagating values at odds with reality in the name of truth, which was henceforth treated as the sharpest weapon of the weak; these values were doomed to failure on the stage of real events, yet they could not, and did not want to, stop anticipating their hour of triumph.

The theological reaction of post-Babylonian Judaism to the experience of slavery crystallized into a cult of exhilaration in defeat. The first real monotheism, which grew from this situation, can therefore be understood first and foremost as a protest theology. It could only be what it was by representing not the ruling religion, but rather the religion of resistance against the ruling power. The purpose of Jewish theocracy was to exalt its own hidden, transcendental kind above the manifest kings of the others. It was only now that Abraham's summotheistic striving for the Highest and Moses' monolatric zeal for the One merged – in an anti-Babylonian and anti-imperial context – to produce a subversive form of devotion critical of, but inevitably also nostalgic for, power. From that point on, it expressed itself as a yearning for superiority over the superior.

The second position in the field of monotheistic conflict has been clearly marked since the appearance of the Christian antithesis to the Jewish thesis. Although the God proclaimed by Paul and the other apostles retains a number of attributes connecting him to his Jewish predecessor, the subversively new Christological emphases lend his image entirely unexpected, even provocative and scandalous aspects.

The crucified God will forever remain a challenge to the worldly understanding of victory and defeat. From a historical perspective, it is decisive that the universalist elements of post-Babylonian Jewish theology were only focused on and invested in an ambitious proselytistic movement as a result of Paul's intervention. The dual event evoked by the names of Jesus of Nazareth and Paul of Tarsus constituted no less than the escape of the One God from the provincial Middle East: it resulted in the alteration of the religious impulse from an ethnically restricted cult to an empire-wide form of telecommunication. The people's apostle could no longer content himself with local Jewish conversations about holy matters. Following a clear strategic instinct, Paul identified the entire Roman Empire, which at the time meant the whole world, as the field of operation for his mission – enough of a reason for Paul to be an idol for lovers of abstract militancy to this day: one could almost call him the first Puritan, the first Jacobin and the first Leninist all rolled into one. Perhaps it is no coincidence that Paul's work is documented primarily in the form of epistles, as that genre testifies to his long-distance apostolic effect more than any other. Even today, the reader can observe in them the gradual formulation of Christianity in the very act of writing.

This shift to the global scale dissolved the conventional folk basis of the faith in a single god. Israel, the first covenant people, could no longer be the sole carrier of the specifically new, Christologically inverted monotheism. Paul's stroke of genius transferred the covenant with God to a new people 'called out' from among the believers of all peoples – this new collective was hence to call itself *ekklesia* or New Israel, and embody the historically unprecedented model of a pneumatic people. It formed the prototype of the *communio*: a large spiritual body joined through baptism. In this collective, following the same Lord now took precedence over tribal lineage and gender. With a grand gesture, the differences between

Jews and Greeks, free men and slaves or men and women were declared meaningless among the 'children of God' (Romans 10:12 and Galatians 3:28). A new associative model, the 'holy community', pushed back the ethnocentrism that, until then, had been the only conceivable option – people were first of all disciples of Christ; their identities as clan members and national comrades were secondary. The underlying belief in the imminent return of the Lord in glory, furthermore, led to a shift of emphasis in which futuristic motives restricted genealogical ones and superseded them *de jure*. God had promised Abraham descendants 'as numerous as the stars in the heavens' after Isaac had been freed; for Paul, however, the model of friendship took precedence over that of succession. Spiritual adoption replaced physical descent.

It was Paul who originated the enthusiastic universalism taken up by later generations of apostles as the motor for their eternally incomplete missionary work. One could use the term 'apostolic integrism' to describe the existential model used by Christ's successors, where the bearer of the message allowed himself to be consumed by his evangelical work. It was not without reason that some claimed one could only call oneself a Christian if one had made a Christian out of at least one other person; through the mission, the way of life became its content. Profane subjectivity had to be exchanged for holy personhood: 'it is no longer I who live, but it is Christ who lives in me' (Galatians 2:20). What looks from the outside like idealistic overexertion is, viewed from the inside, actually the privilege of being allowed to wear oneself out for a great cause, thanks to the most intimate of convictions. Like revenge, the missionary faith approaches the 'utopia of a motivated life'.[14] The believer, it is said, could never develop his zeal for God of his own accord if God's own zeal for his coming kingdom were not working within him. With the Pentecost event, Christianity entered the

---

[14] Sloterdijk, *Zorn und Zeit*, pp. 96f.

realm of high mediality. Subsequently the church became a place of exchange where one could hand over one's old identity and receive a spirited new self.

Only with the advent of Christianity did the zealous form and the universal content of the message grow together into an effective unity – due especially to the irresistible psychodynamic synthesis that was found with the apostolic form of life; the motif of the Holy War, prefigured by devout Jews, was now lifted onto a universal stage. Consequently, the new telematic monotheism had to develop a permanent state of taking the bull by the horns as its own peculiar modus vivendi. Externally it conceived of the world as the reception area for the message it sought to disseminate, while internally it consolidated itself as an employer for kerygmatic and diaconal work – today one would speak of public relations work and therapeutic professions; in this respect the early church anticipated the postmodern service society, whose most important 'product' is the social relations themselves. Finally, as a result of its encounters with the philosophical theology of the Greeks, Christian doctrine also incorporated the provocations of theoretical monotheism, drawing on this fusion to develop an intellectual strength that was to spawn ever-new syntheses of biblical and philosophical ideas over a period of almost eighty generations.

The most important victory of the new religion, however, was in the field of ritual. It was achieved through the transformation of the Jewish Passover feast into the Christian communion – a piratical operation that must be understood as the most world-historically significant example of 'refunctionalization', in the sense propagated by the dramatic artist Brecht. Communion does not simply constitute a strong 'misreading' of the Jewish pattern. It is more than that: its tragic parody. The consequences of this appropriation cannot be stressed enough: it was only through this blasphemous counter-Passover, in which the Son of Man placed himself in the position of the lamb that would normally have been sacrificed (as if he wanted to reveal the secret of that terrible night in Egypt), that Christianity came into possession of an unmistakable maximum stress ritual that guaranteed its participants the most lively form of memoactive empathy – and has by this point been doing so over a period of two millennia.[15] In every mass it is not simply the commemorative meal that is quoted, but rather the intimate memorability of faith itself. Analogously, the feast of Whitsun parodies the handing over of laws at Mount Sinai, which the Jews celebrated fifty days after Passover – as if to prove that the preservation of the law is itself the law.

As far as the question of the 'price of monotheism' in the case of Christianity is concerned, a question often discussed in recent times, we consider it sufficient here to point to two well-known complications. The first relates to the ambivalence of Christianity towards the Jewish mother religion – Paul supplied the formula for this in his letter to the Romans, where he defined the Jews as enemies in terms of the gospel, but as 'beloved for our fathers' sakes' (Romans 11:28) in terms of their chosen status. Even as late as the twentieth century, Paul's thesis was renewed by Pope Pius X, who died in 1914; like many theologians before him, he declared that Judaism had been 'replaced' by Christianity, and that one could consequently no longer 'grant it any continued existence' – which did not form any obstacle to his canonization through Pius XII in 1954. In addition, Christians dealt with Jewish sources in the manner of a hostile take-over – in particular through the appropriation of the Tanach, which, now known as the Old Testament, was annexed, canonized and reinterpreted in the light of Christian needs.

---

[15] Mühlmann, *Jesus überlistet Darwin*. One must also insist that the doctrine of the 'lamb of God' was derived not from the near-sacrifice of Isaac by Abraham, but from the monstrous reinterpretation of the slaughter ritual at Passover.

The second indication concerns the fact that Christianity, which saw itself *in principle* as a religion of love, freedom and warm-hearted inclusion, *in fact* also practised ruthlessness, rigorism and terror on a large scale. The liaison between the Western world of faith and the spirit of Roman law spawned a legally thoroughly regulated church system that was not infrequently attacked, including by critics among its own ranks, as an anti-Christian monstrosity.[16] From the perspective of Eastern Christianity, the Roman power apparatus sometimes seemed like the incarnation of the Antichrist in the shape of a perversely showy corporation. In his late works, Ivan Illich went as far as identifying the estrangement of the church from the gospel as the source of all the estrangements, reifications and dispossessions that had been twisting the lives of modern people for centuries.[17] In defence of Roman Catholicism (though certainly also to prove its beneficial weakening), one should point out that it did not, ultimately, remain indifferent to the wealth of critical reflections: of all the memories of John Paul II, those moments in which the *pontifex maximus* apologized to the whole world for the aberrations of a fallible church's 'sons and daughters' will be among the most lasting.[18]

It is thus all the more understandable that, from the eighteenth century onwards, a post-Christian scepticism spread throughout Europe, which sought to distance itself

---

[16] The most assured representation of Catholic Romanism is to be found in Hans Küng's magnum opus *Das Christentum* [Christianity] (Munich, 1994), in the third section of the historical part, which, under the title 'The Roman Catholic Paradigm of the Middle Ages', shows in particular – like a book within a book – the process of 'Romanization at the expense of Catholic identity' with reference to centralization, juridicization, politicization, militarization and clericalization.

[17] David Cayley, *The Rivers North of the Future: The Testament of Ivan Illich* (Toronto: House of Anansi Press, 2005).

[18] Especially in the extensive request for forgiveness on 12 March 2000.

from the extremes of zealous faith, often even from faith as a whole. The alienation from the church prevalent on the continent today does not, therefore, merely show the hallmarks of institutional criticism and anti-dogmatism; the proponents of a purely secular way of life frequently launch open attacks. Some resolute heirs of the Enlightenment hold the conviction that Christianity still deserves to be showered with the most vicious blasphemies for centuries to come. Did Robespierre not declare in his speech before the assembly in 1794 that priests are to morality what charlatans are to medicine?[19] The churches and their dogmas have had to put up with caricatures and malice for 200 years – without being able, as they still were in the Middle Ages, to escape from 'this world' through a fundamental withdrawal. On critical days, this anti-clerical sentiment is released in such satirical statements as this one: 'The existence of Christians proves the non-existence of God.'[20] The fact that some Christians today can even laugh at such jokes shows that they are capable of learning.

With the advent of Islam, the third exclusive monotheism appeared on the scene. Its establishment was defined by the fact that it viewed itself emphatically as the latest and most perfect manifestation of the Abrahamic one god complex. Islam took its late arrival as its most precious spiritual chance, as it claimed the advantage of seeing and correcting the errors, both alleged and real, of the two preceding monotheisms. This is why Muslim clerics refer to the founder of their religion as the 'seal of the prophet'. The idea of correction in the process of monotheistic revelations is constitutive for Islam, as it permits it to

---

[19] Maximilien Robespierre, 'Rapport sur les idées religieuses et morales' (7 May 1794) in *Histoire parlementaire de la Révolution française*, ed. Philippe-Joseph-Benjamin Buchez and Pierre-Célestin Roux-Lavergne (Paris: Paulin, 1834–8), vol XXXII, pp. 353ff.
[20] Louis Scutenaire, *Mes inscriptions 1943–1944* (Paris: Allia, 1982).

make a virtue out of necessity by converting the deficit of non-originality into the advantage of a later clarification. Just as the Christian message before it could only come about through a partial abrogation, a corrective revocation of Jewish teachings (literary critics would add: through a severe misreading), the Islamic revelation presupposes the partial abrogation of the two older versions of monotheism. (Here this misreading of its two predecessors is taken to a spectacular level; yet it is precisely the success of Islam that shows that the adepts of this new holy book had more important things to do than draw on the sources of existing cults in a philologically correct fashion.) Consequently the religion of the Qur'an, like that of the New Testament, was substantially characterized by a position of theological contrast; its first front stood in the tradition of the Jewish and Christian zealots who waged war against the gods and idols of their polytheistic surroundings, while the second opposed the Jews and Christians directly. The former were accused of being frivolous and hypocritical, as they did not even take their own prophets seriously, while the latter were presented with the charge of falsely declaring the prophet Jesus 'the Son of God' in their deludedness, whereas all true knowledge of God, according to Islam, begins with the realization that the Highest is alone for all eternity and has no child. The pathos of the Islamic thesis of God's solitary position is based primarily on the polemic against the Christian doctrine of the Trinity, which was regarded with suspicion as a form of tritheism.

As a corrective of Christology, and simultaneously its functional equivalent, Islam developed a prophetology intended to lend the new religion the vigour of legitimacy. It would not only be the Arab recipients who would find the idea that God had sent a human ambassador to those willing to embrace this faith more convincing than the suggestion that this ambassador was God himself, albeit in a second mode. In that case, admittedly, the prophet would have to be given an incomparably elevated status that would soon reach dizzying heights. This demanded no less than a doctrine of *inlibration*, God's embodiment in book form, which in turn called for the dogma of the dictation of that book by the angel of God. Obviously, such a directive could only be received by a single pure, devoted medium – from a Catholic perspective, this suggests an analogy between Mohammed and Mary. Devotees of the virgin will have an idea what Muslims might mean if they occasionally speak of a 'virgin birth of the Qur'an'.[21]

Islam was also dependent on the creation of a maximum stress myth. It produced this in the form of the duty for all Muslims to go on a pilgrimage to Mecca: the climaxes of this gruelling undertaking lie in the pilgrim's personal participation in the stoning of the devil and the slaughter of a sacrificial animal. Thanks to these forms of 'deep play' (as one sometimes calls deeply involving ritual acts), Islamic doctrines are connected to a heavily emotional memoactive engram.[22] Needless to say, Islam could never have survived through one and a half millennia if the dramatizations of its teachings had not made such a lasting impression.

While the monotheistic escalation in Paul's case had triggered the shift from a defensive to an offensive universalism, the Islamic escalation led to the further development of offensive universalism from the missionary to the military-political form of expansion. The beginning of Islam was already triumphant; it managed to hurdle the phase of *ecclesia oppressa*[23] at the first attempt. In the case

---

[21] See, for example, I. S. Hussain, *The Qur'an and Modernism. Beyond Science and Philosophy* (Lahore, 2000), pp. 1f.: 'The Qur'an: An Immaculate Conception'.
[22] Mühlmann, *Jesus überlistet Darwin*.
[23] According to the narrative scheme *ecclesia oppressa, ecclesia militans, ecclesia triumphans* – from the church under pressure to the fighting church, then from the fighting to the triumphant church – used in church history to summarize the political fate of Christianity between the death of Christ and the Constantinian shift.

of Christianity, the metaphysics of the strong sender developed further by Paul had resulted in the belief that the crucified one was God's divine envoy and equal; the apostles could follow on from him as second-degree messengers. The same sender formula was used by the Muslims in order to honour a prophet who combined the roles of spiritual spokesman and military commander in a single person. In both cases, the strong sender on the other side was tied to a privileged mediator on this side, whose path was to be followed and made useful by countless later mediators of faith – the systemic point of departure for all those phenomena placed in such categories as clergy and clerical rule. While Paul had occasionally referred to the faithful as the athletes of Christ (1 Corinthians 17:24f.) – a metaphor that manifested itself in Christian monastic life with the fury of the literal – the militant followers of Allah viewed themselves as voluntary recruits in a holy expansion campaign. From a distance, they remind one of the Puritan cavalry of Oliver Cromwell, an army for whom praying and fighting were as close together as they were for the religiously aroused warriors of the early Caliphate. The social form of the new movement was the *ummah*, the non-tribal commune to which one was admitted not by birth, but through the recitation of the creed of allegiance (*shahadah*) to Allah and his prophet before witnesses. The explosive expansion of Islam in the two centuries following the death of the prophet shows what powers were unleashed through the unexpected alliance between the clan system and universalism.

Islam in its original form owes its dynamics to the circumstance that in its case – in contrast to the initially oppositional, state-critical stance of Christianity – religious and politico-military impulses were practically acting in unison from the outset. This did not prevent Islam from developing a surrealism of its own kind – unlike Augustinian Christianity, however, it never managed to formulate a doctrine of the two kingdoms. It sought to project the opposition between religious space and worldliness outwards, so to speak, and distinguish between the 'house of Islam' and the 'house of war'. Rousseau still praised the close complicity of religion and state policy in Mohammed's legacy, attempting to imitate it in his own plans for a 'bourgeois revolution'. Going on these indications, the religion of the revolutionaries of 1794 was intended to establish a post-Christian non-differentiation between state and 'church' in order to force – in France, the cradle of totalitarian temptations – a comprehensive identification of citizens with their community. This endeavour was foiled not only by the liberalism of the enlightened bourgeoisie, but also by the resistance of deep-seated Catholic traditions. The author of the *Contrat social* showed foresight and logical consistency in attacking Christianity as a hotbed of political disloyalty and social divisions. Whoever speaks of totalitarianism today should never forget that it acted out its dress rehearsal as a revolutionary civil religion. Rousseau had been its prophet, and his faithful disciple Robespierre followed in his footprints in presenting himself as the first caliph of a modern republic of conviction.

3

The battle fronts

Having presented the main candidates on the field of monotheistic faith and zeal (a fourth, the Communism expanding in the nineteenth century, does not require consideration at this point), it is not very difficult to subject the potential and actual confrontations between the monotheisms to systematic examination. Gaining the freest view of the field requires not a historical report, but rather a combinatorial scheme detailing all the formal possibilities of confrontation between the protagonists. In the following structural exercise – which, I hope, will not shock readers with its methodical callousness – I shall present twelve, or perhaps eighteen, basic possibilities of inter-monotheistic and intra-monotheistic formation of fronts, pointing here and there to the historical or diachronic contents of the synchronously schematized constellations. Their order is arbitrary and does not convey anything about the historical or moral weight of the individual figures in the conflicts. As I shall begin with the Christian positions, it is fitting that the oldest and most harmful manifestation of inter-monotheistic polemic should be mentioned first.

The first figure of confrontation on the inter-monotheistic field is *Christian anti-Judaism* (1), whose founding document, the proto-apostle's letter to the Romans, has already been mentioned above. One of its oldest sources is also the Gospel of John, which already displays the most vehement anti-Jewish sentiment – here the Jews are openly condemned as the 'children of Satan' and viewed as part of a counter-world that has been rejected. Needless to say, such statements are more than simply the darkest blot on the history of the world's favourite religion; beyond that, they also make it clear what price was paid for this new idea of the Messiah. From an evolution-dynamic perspective, religious anti-Judaism constitutes a special case within a more general law, namely that the inception of an innovative 'spiritual movement' will inevitably leave behind slower groups, whose delayed or reluctant manner is taken as a ruinous sign by those already ahead. As the conservatives of the old covenant, the Jews were to embody this law and suffer under it, just as they looked back upon the Egyptians and the idolaters of Canaan as allegedly spiritually backward. As the history of the Christian hostility towards Jews fills entire libraries, archives of villainy that taught generations of academics to doubt Christianity, if not humanity at large, there is no further need to speak about it in the context of a formal enumeration – except for the conceptual criticism that one often describes these phenomena completely mechanically with the word 'anti-Semitism', which still gives the absurd fabrications of the political racism of the nineteenth century too much credence.

The next figure is that of *Christian anti-Islamism* (2), whose beginnings can be traced back to the Byzantine reactions to the Arab-Islamic attacks of the seventh and eighth centuries. The Byzantine Empire had already lost two-thirds of its territories and half of its population to the Islamic conquerors by this point. In the High Middle Ages, the denigration of Islam was commonplace in Europe. When Dante wrote the twenty-eighth Canto of *Inferno*, which depicts the prophet Mohammed, together with the sowers of scandal and schism, being hacked to pieces by a sword-wielding devil for all eternity, he was most likely able to draw on the Islamophobic clichés of his time without having to rely on any inspiration himself – if one leaves aside the *commedia*'s typical schema of analogy between the manner of blasphemy and the mode of infernal punishment. A further document of Christian Islamophobia from the early fifteenth century was made famous by the speech given by Pope Benedict XVI in Regensburg in September 2006, in which he quoted the statement – or rather the sigh – of the unhappy emperor, Manuel II Palaiologos (whose daughter had once sat in the harem of the enemy as they besieged Byzantium), that the prophet Mohammed had added nothing but evil and inhumanity to Christian revelation.

Next we should mention *Christian anti-Paganism* (3), a prototype for all monotheistic religious polemic. The Christian opposition to the *pagani*, i.e. the followers of the 'backward' religion of the villages and fields in the Roman Empire (like the opposition to the *gentiles*, the yet unconverted foreign peoples), was determined by two factors: firstly, it stemmed in a more indirect manner from the traditional Jewish rejection of the idolatrous and cultic religions that had previously dominated. Secondly, it developed from the urbane design of the 'God's people' project as conceived by Paul, with a clear imperial instinct in analogy to the Roman–Hellenistic ecumenical model. In this project the new figure of God, designed for the maximum mediality and transportability, inevitably came into great conflict with anything that recalled the magical circles of the older rural relics and local cults. The entire history of Christianity is thus characterized by a polemical tension between itself and all forms of folk religion with its magical-polytheistic dispositions, extending to the atrocities of the inquisition trials and extermination of witches – a tension that also permitted compromises, such as the cult of saints and relics and other manifestations of the semi-heathen, reterritorialized, folkloric and national-Catholic religion of the people.

In the next round we encounter *Islamic anti-Christianism* (4) and *Islamic anti-Judaism* (5). As much as Islam was aware of its later historical position in relation to the two other exclusively monotheistic movements, and consequently saw fit to cultivate the knowledge of those connections, it nonetheless insisted on displaying its specific differences from the earlier religions of the book. I am not sure whether Christian Delacampagne is right to speak of a 'radically anti-Jewish logic'[1] informing Muslim culture from its beginnings to the present day. One can, however, diagnose a far-reaching ambivalence towards the Jewish legacy, for which the history of both ideas and actions in the corresponding field of conflict provides ample evidence. In fact, an emphatic distancing from Judaism can be traced back to Mohammed's Medina period. Not only was Jerusalem replaced by Mecca as the direction of prayer; there were also 'cleansings and massacres' of Jewish citizens – I have taken these two qualifications from Hans Küng's very empathetic and well-disposed monograph on the third of the Abrahamic religions.[2] Whether one considers it constitutive or conjunctural, anti-Jewish sentiment in Islam has been reinforced by the texts of such writers as the Egyptian ideologue Sayyid Qutb (1906–66), who held the view that the West was waging a war of conquest against the Islamic world, and that this war was controlled primarily by Jewish interests. Such agitated interpretations of the time have recently been augmented by the loud, apocalyptic Muslim sects that are omnipresent in Arab pop culture and burn with anticipation for the extermination of Judaism as if it were a salvation-historical event.

While Jews and Christians, as 'people of the book', were treated with greater tolerance, even a certain respect in classical Islam (especially when they lived as *dhimmi*, wards who were protected under Islamic law and paid the

---

[1] Christian Delacampagne, *Islam et Occident. Les raisons d'un conflit* (Paris: Presses Universitaires de France, 2003), p. 27.
[2] Hans Küng, *Der Islam. Geschichte, Gegenwart, Zukunft* [Islam: Past, Present and Future] (Munich and Zurich: Piper, 2006), p. 152.

poll tax), the monotheistic polemic against all that was alien or archaic showed itself all the more virulently in *Islamic anti-Paganism* (6). Unlike its Christian counterpart, this was not directed at the country-dwellers with polytheistic origins, whom believers in the city and the rest of the empire viewed as a thorn in their side. This time its impulses came from the religiously inflamed nomadic cultures of the desert, aimed at the confusion of the cities with all their cultic polyvalence, wealth of images and architectural excesses. There was an attempt, not entirely without substance, to attribute the attacks of 11 September 2001 to the imaginary idea of the original Islam (although contemporary Islamic extremism seems most prevalent in cities and among students). It is no secret that certain passages in the Qur'an openly urge believers not only to kill polytheists (Sura 2:191, Sura 9:5, etc.), but also to destroy their cities and towers if they refuse to accept the holy word (Sura 17:58: 'And there is no city that we would not ravage before the day of resurrection'). One of the sources of religiously coded anti-urbanism in Islam was pointed out by Régis Debray in his uncovering of the close connection between original monotheism and the experience of living in the desert: 'God is a nomad who has been extended to the heavens, remembering his dunes.'[3]

The next item on the list of inter-monotheistic conflict areas is *Jewish anti-Christianism* (7) – a position presumably connected to a wide range of historical realities that were not, to the best of our knowledge, explicitly documented. There is at least evidence, however, that the reactionary rabbinical factions in Judaism prayed in their synagogues for the destruction of the 'Nazarenes' from the second century AD onwards: 'May their names be

---

[3] Régis Debray, *Einführung in die Mediologie* [Introduction to Mediology] (Bern Stuttgart and Vienna: Hauph Verlag, 2003), p. 98.

struck from the Book of Life.'[4] Such polemics are undoubtedly more than simply the inversions of Christian anti-Judaism. If, on the one hand, Christianity inevitably saw the mere existence of Judaism as a provocation, as the Jews' continued adherence to their traditional doctrine could only mean a harsh rejection of the Christian message, then conversely, on the other hand, the new faith of Christians in Jesus as the envoy of God was destined to be met with more or less open disapproval among the Jews. In more recent times, Jewish authors writing from a religion-psychological perspective have occasionally proposed that Christianity is fundamentally regressive in comparison to Judaism, as it exchanged the more mature belief in a life under the law for an illusory bond with a messiah who had 'come'. One can see just how far such anti-Christian polemic in Jewish sources can extend in a book by the psychoanalysts Béla Grunberger and Pierre Dessuant entitled *Narzissmus, Christentum, Antisemitismus*,[5] in which the authors suggest that there is a continuum of malign Christian narcissism leading straight from Jesus to Hitler. Although the authors stepped onto the field of universal polemic with this claim, there was no scandal; those under attack simply shook their heads. Here one could observe with bafflement how psychoanalysis was being appropriated by a zealous Judaism without boundaries.

As far as *Jewish anti-Islamism* (8) is concerned, its historical manifestations have remained faint and presumably little-examined. Whatever their nature may have been, they would have been balanced out by occasional Jewish–Islamic alliances, which can be traced back to the time of the crusades. At any rate, the anti-Arab and

---

[4] F. E. Peters, *The Monotheists. Jews, Christians and Muslims in Conflict and Competition*, vol. I: *The Peoples of God* (Princeton and Oxford: Princeton University Press, 2003), p. 161.
[5] Stuttgart: Klett-Cotta, 2000.

anti-Muslim attacks of the New York 'hate preacher' Meir Kahan (1932–90) only expressed a marginal position within Judaism. The ideal and real manifestations of *Jewish anti-Paganism* (9), on the other hand, are far clearer: they lead us to the exophobic origins of any exclusive monotheism. One can justify it by pointing to its defensive character. If Judaism had not withdrawn behind the 'fence of the law', it would hardly have survived the countless trials of history. On the other hand, the antithetical relationship between the Jewish faith and the conventions of those with other beliefs in the Middle East would never have grown into the vicious conflict that has meanwhile become familiar without this. One could say that the division of mankind into Jews and gentiles (*goyim*) still common today (a distinction that seems to pass the lips of German Sunday speakers especially easily) highlights aspects of a very old attitude, both fearful and contemptuous, towards the followers of other gods and depraved cults.

Finally one must take into account the possibility and reality of internal schisms, which extended the polemical range with three further positions: Christian *anti-Christianism* (10), Islamic *anti-Islamism* (11) and Jewish *anti-Judaism* (12). As far as the first of these is concerned, we primarily recall the deep gulf between the Christian confessions from the century of the Reformation onwards (prefigured by numerous dogmatically and politically motivated schisms in early church history). Nonetheless, this is only one of many manifestations of the potential for intra-Christian conflict. Like all monotheisms, the Christian variety is no stranger to the tension between the rigorist and laxist interpretations of the scriptures on the one hand, and the chronic friction between orthodox and heretical tendencies on the other. In the case of Islam, one naturally thinks of the breaking away of the Shia, which, according to the contemporary Sunni leader Abu Mus'ab al Zarkawi, has as little to do with Islam as Judaism with Christianity, 'which are likewise based on the same scripture'.[6] In the case of Judaism, as well as the Cabbalistic and mystical deviations from orthodoxy, the most obvious choice would be the opposition between the legalistic and messianic schools of thought. The schism between the conservative and the liberal synagogue is also not without certain polemogenic effects.

This overview outlines the twelve main battle fronts that could transpire from an identitary, collective-forming and polemogenic use of the three monotheistic syntheses. If one considers possible two-against-one coalitions, a further three figures can be added to the list: Christians and Muslims against Jews (13), Jews and Muslims against Christians (14), and Jews and Christians against Muslims (15). I shall refrain from supplying historical indications of such alliances.

With reference to real and virtual religious history, one should also note the development of three atheisms corresponding to the three monotheisms, a process that took place with evolutionary necessity. In order to understand this, one must acknowledge the fact that atheism does not usually stem from a context-free logical examination of the existence or non-existence of God. It practically always comes from idiosyncratic negations of particular theistic tenets and their organized cultic contexts. In this sense, atheism constitutes a regional phenomenon. We must therefore take into account a *Christian atheism* and its damnation by orthodox Christians (16), then *Islamic atheism* and its damnation by Islamic zealots (17) and *Jewish atheism* with its damnation by pious Jews (18). The term 'damnation' here encompasses the darkest of meanings: for Thomas Aquinas, falling away from the Christian faith was a crime that deserved to be punished with

---

[6] Excerpts from the 'Letter to Bin Laden and al Zawahiri' in *Al Quaida. Texte des Terrors*, edited with a commentary by Gilles Kepel and Jean-Pierre Milelli (Munich, 2006), p. 459. English edition: *Al Qaeda in Its Own Words*, trans. Pascale Ghazaleh (Cambridge, Mass.: Belknap Press, 2008).

death; even at the end of the seventeenth century, the constitution of the Puritan theocracy in Massachusetts stated that the crime of atheism called for the death penalty; in the Islamic republic of Pakistan, non-believers and followers of other faiths can still be sentenced to death on charges of apostasy and blasphemy. Admittedly Rousseau, the totalitarian prophet of the Enlightenment, also proposed the death penalty for those who broke away from the 'civil religion' – and even in the enlightened Western 'societies' of today, there is no shortage of examples showing how readily the civil-religiously committed centrists begin a witch hunt whenever individuals blaspheme against the liberal consensus: a witch hunt whose practitioners happily take into account the social death of their victim. It is much rarer to encounter an abstract atheism free of any presuppositions, one that adopts a stance against the historical theisms as a whole – for example in the *Treatise on the Three Impostors* (these being Moses, Jesus and Mohammed) from the eighteenth century, whose anonymous author, inspired by Spinoza, takes the common Enlightenment doctrine of clerical fraud to the point of prophet fraud, even fraud by the religious founders – and actually implies that these founding fathers were not only deceivers, but also the first to be deceived. The recent case of the biologist Richard Dawkins, whose book *The God Delusion* (2006) is a monument to the eternal shallowness of Anglican atheism, shows how avowed deniers of God can in turn be duped by their own zeal.

If, having completed our brief rundown, we cast a glance at the conflict area as a whole, two concluding observations seem inescapable: firstly, one can see that the classical monotheisms clearly did not make the most of their polemogenic potential. Even if one believes that the inter- and intra-monotheistic struggles cost too many lives anyway, studying the formally prefigured likelihood of different enmities between these religions in a structural overview reveals just how far the historical reality fell short of the script's possibilities. It should be clear why this insufficiency was beneficial to mankind, which would otherwise have fought many more battles.

Secondly, we should not neglect to mention the non-combatant observers on the edges of the tripolemic field, who have always cast astonished and disapproving glances at the warlike formations of the participants. In their own way, these also belong to the scene of the battling monotheisms. For them, admittedly, the state of consciousness among the 'common people' is decisive, as the masses' blissful lack of opinion (as God is too enormous a subject) or principles (as fundamental issues always lead to over-exertion) makes them keep their distance from the tiring theatre of hyper-motivation among the faithful and the chosen.

4

The campaigns

If it is accurate to characterize the classical monotheisms as vehicles of zealous universalism, this inevitably raises the question of their world strategies. Naturally, each of these religions has a well-developed reality of life or, as Ivan Illich puts it, a vernacular side in which the charm of non-zealous, everyday religious life enforced by cult and tradition can take effect. As is well known, Chateaubriand celebrated the 'beauties of the Christian religion',[1] and Jewish and Islamic apologists could equally have dealt with the attractions of their religions. As well as the aesthetic merits, such defences would have emphasized above all the moral or social achievements that unfolded within the local communes in more or less impressive ways. As open as we may be to the charms of the monotheistic forms of life in the 'rear line', however (without overlooking its compulsive aspects, for example the Islamic custom of circumcision among young girls, ultimately motivated simply by a rule-obsessed attachment to a malign tradition, coupled with the need to pass on one's own lack of freedom), all three must primarily be defined as front-line

---

[1] François-René de Chateaubriand, *Le génie du christianisme* (Paris, 1802). English translation: *The Genius of Christianity or The Spirit and Beauty of the Christian Religion*, trans. Charles I. White (New York: Howard Fertig, 1975).

religions owing to their polemical beginnings. The fact that their offensive potential sometimes lay dormant for centuries under certain historical conditions does not change the expansive orientation of the programmes. Each of the monotheisms has its own specific quality of 'world-taking', to use a term coined by Carl Schmitt in a different context. The truth is that the One and Only, though first discovered in the regional cult, inevitably ends up being promoted as a god with imposing worldly representation and increasing claims to sovereignty. Because of its predication on a concept of God that emphasizes the uniqueness and omnipotence of the Highest, religious universalism produces surpluses of meaning that erupt in encroachments of monotheistic communes on their political and cultic environments.

In the following, I shall distinguish between three main forms of expansion that are evident in the historical development of monotheistic campaigns. The first, that of theocratic sovereignism, which came to exert a defining influence on Judaism throughout its many times and spaces, has predominantly defensive and separatist characteristics, while the second and third forms, namely expansion through missionary activity and through the Holy War, show a clearly offensive approach, one that also encompassed such means as persuasion, coercion and subjugation, even open blackmail ('Baptism or death!', 'Qur'an or death!'). I do not think any formal proof is required that the latter two forms are not atypical of the two more extroverted monotheisms.

One can only speak of a Jewish campaign in the limited, even paradoxical, sense that the surpluses of meaning found in post-exile monotheism show a clear anti-Babylonian, and later also anti-Hellenic, anti-Roman and generally anti-imperial, thrust. One cannot, on the other hand, speak of any missionary expansion or proselytistic dynamic in Judaism as a whole. The post-Babylonian theology of Judaism is sovereignist in so far as it claims a supreme position for the god of the enslaved people – a provocation that became unforgettable especially through the book of Genesis, whose final version was produced in the post-exile era. The basic position of Judaism in relation to the rest of the world, however, remained a separatist one in so far as it refused any form of cultic communality with the other religious peoples and evaded any ecumenical mixture or levelling out – an approach that, especially in the families of the Jewish priests, the *kohanim*, maintained a high degree of biological stability over millennia.[2] It proves the effectiveness of a closed religious community as a 'selective genetic force'.[3] The necessity of an outward missionary shift was only conceded for relatively short periods – it is perhaps no coincidence that the only proselytistic episode in the history of Judaism was in the time directly before the messianic sect of Jesuans broke away from the main movement (from *c.*150 BC to AD 50). For the majority of its historical existence, however, Judaism occupied a position that can best be described as defensive universalism. With this self-enclosed stance, the people of Israel produced – initially on the basis of tribal and small-state forms of life, later (after what Harold Bloom terms the 'Roman holocaust') under the conditions of exile and dispersion – a massive theological surplus that would have been sufficient for a large empire, even though the originators of these teachings could not even rely on their subsistence as a people on their own territory for many centuries. By following the notion of living under the eyes of a watchful god, the Jewish people developed a sensorium for the counter-observation of this god, through which a theologically tinged, eccentric positionality (concentrated in the idea of the covenant) became second nature.

---

[2] See Dean Hamer, *The God Gene: How Faith Is Hardwired into Our Genes* (New York: Anchor, 2005), ch. 10, 'The DNA of the Jews'.
[3] Ibid.

If, in spite of all our reservations, it were permissible to speak of a Jewish campaign, this expression could only refer to what Leo Baeck termed, in *Das Wesen des Judentums* [The Nature of Judaism] (1905), the 'struggle for self-preservation'. Certainly, according to Baeck, it is impossible to conceive of Judaism as a whole without the 'force of instruction and conversion', but this potential was only able to take effect in an introverted and defensive direction during almost 2,000 years of diaspora. 'People understood that *mere existence can already be a declaration*, a sermon to the world... The mere fact that one existed posited some meaning... Self-preservation was experienced as preservation through God.'[4] One Christian author exaggerated these statements to the most obvious extent by declaring that, for him, the continued existence of Judaism in the world of today constitutes no less than a historical proof of God's existence. Advocates of evolutionist neuro-rhetoric would say that the longevity of Judaism proves the precise vertical duplicability of the memoactive rituals practised among this people. As Judaism invested its religious surpluses of meaning in its self-preservation as a people and a ritual community, its physical existence became charged with metaphysical ideas that amounted to the fulfilment of a mission – one more reason why the physical attack on Judaism can go hand in hand with the desire for its spiritual and moral eradication.

Formally speaking, the relationship between Judaism and the two religions that followed it could be viewed as a spiritual prefiguration of the asymmetrical war. Henry Kissinger supplied the latter's strategic formula in 1969 with the observation that the guerrillas win if they do not lose, whereas the regular troops lose if they do not win. The Jewish position corresponds to that of a guerrilla movement that takes the non-defeat it constantly achieves

---

[4] Leo, Baeck, *Das Wesen des Judentums*, 10th edition (Wiesbaden, 1991), p. 290.

as a necessary, albeit inadequate, condition for its victory. By securing its survival, it creates the preconditions for its provisional – and who knows, perhaps one day even its ultimate – success. The 'preservation of Judaism' takes place, as Leo Baeck notes with prophetic pathos, according to the 'strict laws of life' in a historical selection process. 'History chooses, for it demands a decision; it becomes the grand selection among humans.' 'When the gravity of circumstances calls upon humanity, it is often only the few who are left . . . The remainder is the justification for history.'[5] Hence the real Jewish campaign resembles a swift gallop through many times and realms with heavy losses. This *anabasis* of the just has the form of a test undergone by each new generation. Here, a minority is filtered out from within a minority in order to continue the monotheistic adventure in its original form, life under the law and behind the 'fence around the doctrine'[6] as unadulteratedly as possible. Here, the fundamental paradox of this religious structure, the fixation of the universal god on a single people, is prevented, with all its practitioners' power, from unfolding.

The state of Israel proclaimed in 1948 secularized the motif of tested survival. It presents itself as the political form of a 'society' of immigrants that claims (after the people's 'return' to the region of its former historical existence) an additional, discreetly transcendental significance for its physical existence. To many Jews, founding a state of their own seemed the only possible way of securing their future survival after the Shoa. As one of the conflict parties in the permanent crisis in the Middle East, Israel is paying a high price for this. In this role, it is inevitably losing a large part of the moral advantages it could still claim as long as it perceived itself as a dispersed, suffering community. The number of those still willing to accompany Israel through the complications of its new position

---
[5] Ibid., p. 279.
[6] Ibid., pp. 294f.

is not especially great. In this position, it suffers from the compulsion to show strength just as it formerly suffered from its ability to survive mistreatment. Here too, there is no doubt as to the primacy of the defensive. Let us bear in mind that this hypothesis concerns Israel's reason of state, not the obstructed universalism of Jewish religiosity.

One can speak far more directly of a Christian campaign, as its appearance was accompanied by a shift towards offensive universalism. Within it, one finds the paradoxes of monotheistic system formation still suppressed in Judaism being developed bit by bit. Its appearance on the stage of earth-shattering forces teaches us that ideas of this level embody themselves in autopoietic processes that, on the basis of their results, one reads as success stories. The administrators of the *imperium Romanum* realized early on how dangerous the Christian provocation was when they suppressed the new religion and its missionary efforts in several waves of persecution, while generally leaving the non-missionary Jews in peace. During the period of repression, the Christians remained true to their non-violent, ecstatically passive stance. They only formed alliances that resorted to violence once their faith had become the state religion. One can certainly understand what historians critical of the church mean when they date Christianity's own Fall to the moment when it began to cohabit with worldly power.

The essence of Christianity's historical successes can be expressed in a trivial observation: the majority of people today use the Christian calendar, or refer to it as an external guideline in so far as they follow other counting systems that define our current year as 2007 *post Christum natum* – which corresponds roughly to the Jewish year 5767 or the Islamic year 1428. Only few contemporaries realize that, in doing so, they are acting in relation to an event that marks a caesura in the 'history of truth'. In this counting system, the year AD 0 reminds us of the moment at which the 'world' became the broadcasting area for a radically inclusive message. This message was that all people, in accordance with their common nature as creatures, should view themselves as members of a single commune created by God, destroyed by human sin and restored by the Son of God. If understood, this news should result in the dissolution of the enmities that arise among individuals and groups; it would also annul the hermetic self-enclosure of the different cultures and make all collectives follow a shared ideal of sublime justice.

Morally speaking, this was one of the best things humanity had ever heard – which did not, admittedly, prevent a number of the worst conflicts from growing out of the rivalries between those groups who sought to secure the privilege of bringing the good news to the non-believers. In noting that 'the world changed into a site of cockfights for apostles',[7] the subtle reactionary Dávila recognized one of the primary aspects of monotheistic conflicts. He underestimated the potency of such 'cockfights' for making history, however. In fact, this 'history' results from the project of the monotheistic will to total communication. From an internal point of view, it means the process of opening all peoples up to the news of the One God, whose portrait is differentiated into a trinity. All that has gone before now sinks down into aeons past, and only retains validity in so far as it can be interpreted as a preparation for the gospel. Whereas human life until then had hardly consisted of anything except obedience to the cycles of nature and the rise and fall of empires, it would now be integrated into a purposeful process. The world is set in historical motion, in the stricter sense of the word, from the moment in which everything that happens is supposed to be governed by a single principle. What we call history is the campaign of the human race to achieve

---

[7] Nicolás Gómez Dávila, *Das Leben ist die Guillotine der Wahrheiten. Ausgewählte Sprengsätze* [Life Is a Guillotine of Truths. Selected Explosives], ed. Martin Mosebach (Frankfurt am Main, 2006), p. 28.

consenting unity under a god common to all. In this sense, Leo Baeck was right that there is 'no monotheism without world history'.[8] This concept of history presupposes that Christianity is the executive organ of messianic work. In fact, the significance of the messianic only becomes genuinely clear once it is fulfilled through the evangelical. Messianism *post Christum natum* testifies not only to the Jewish non-observance of the Christian caesura, it also shows that, despite the arrival of the good news, there is still enough room for the expectation of new good, even among Christians. Whether there can and should be a collection of the good news of new good in a Newer Testament remains to be seen.

The special role of Paul in overturning the Jewish privilege of sole access to the One and Highest has already been mentioned in the section on the battle formations. Characteristically, there has been no lack of exegetes among the Jewish theologians of recent times who no longer see Paul as a mere traitor, the role he has always embodied for the majority of Jewish commentators. He is increasingly being acknowledged as the zealot who, in bringing the universalist potential of the post-Babylonian Jewish doctrine of God into the world through an ingenious popularization, actually showed that he took the fundamental clerical vocation of the Jewish people seriously. An author such as Ben-Chorin states that even Jews should ultimately applaud the fact that Israel's monotheistic zeal proved infectious for other peoples of the world – albeit at the price that the Christians were lamentably deluded in their play with the messianic fire.[9] The shift to the global scale remained irrevocably tied to the Christian caesura. In his *Letter to the Magnesians* (10:3–4), Ignatius of Antioch, an author of the early second century,

---

[8] Baeck, *Das Wesen des Judentums*, p. 264.
[9] Schalom Ben-Chorin, *Paulus: der Völkerapostel in jüdischer Sicht* [Paul: the People's Apostle From a Jewish Perspective] (Munich, 1997).

stated in no uncertain terms that Judaism leads to Christianity, not vice versa. In this thesis one hears the voice of the resolute cleric who, beyond the martyrdom he aspired to for his own person, demanded and predicted the triumph of the Christian cause on a grand scale.[10]

Under the magnifying glass of success, the dark sides of zealous monotheism also develop into world powers. The zealotic militancy of the early Christians soon came into severe conflict with the circumstance that these devout few were inevitably faced with a vast majority of people to whom the faith of this new sect meant nothing. The zealots took revenge by branding those who did not share their faith 'infidels'. The latter's unperturbed insistence on their previous ideas was thus declared a spiritual crime with grave metaphysical consequences – especially when they chose to decline Christianity's offer after extensive reflection. This is why, from its earliest days, the message of salvation has been accompanied by an escort of threats predicting the worst for unbelievers. Certainly the gospel speaks of wanting to bring blessings to all sides; but Christian militantism has wished the curse of heaven upon the unconverted from its inception. On the one hand, Paul writes to the Corinthians: 'If I speak in the tongues of men and of angels, but have not love, I am only a resounding gong or a clanging cymbal' (1 Corinthians 13:1). On the other hand, in the second epistle to the Thessalonians (1:8–9) – whose authenticity is not uncontested – one can already observe the apocalyptic shadow that grows with the spreading of the message: when the Lord is revealed from heaven in blazing fire, 'He will punish those who do not know God and do not obey the gospel of our Lord Jesus. They will be punished with everlasting destruction and shut out from the presence of the Lord.' So the writings of the people's apostle already promote a love that,

---

[10] This passage contains what is considered the earliest appearance (*c.* AD 115) of the word *christianismós*, which was formed in analogy to the older term *judaismós*.

if not requited, turns into scorn and lust for extermination. The physiognomy of the offensive universalist monotheisms is characterized by the determination of the preachers to make themselves fearsome in the name of the Lord. Possibly this corresponds to a rule of universalist religious communication, namely that every gospel must inevitably cast a dysangelic shadow in the course of its proclamation. Thus the non-acceptance of its truths in fact becomes a dangerous indicator of imminent disaster. The message divides the world as a whole into the unequal halves of church and world. The Christian offensive's ambition to define that whole cannot be fulfilled without excluding 'this world' from the holy community. What constitutes a paradox in logical terms, however, amounts to horror in moral terms.

One can therefore agree – not without a grain of salt – with Alfred N. Whitehead when he reaches the following conclusion in his lectures on the philosophy of religion (Boston, 1926): 'On the whole, the Gospel of love was turned into a Gospel of fear. The Christian world was composed of terrified populations.'[11] One should append the question as to whether it was really a matter of turning a fundamentally good thing into its opposite, or rather an ambivalence that was present from the start. In this case, the motives of Christian missionary successes should be interpreted more critically than is generally the case in official church histories. They should no longer be attributed exclusively to the infectious effects of evangelical proclamations, which undeniably had an innate tendency towards improving the world's moral climate at first. They would then be attributable equally to the threats used to enslave intimately those who received them. That would

---

[11] Alfred N. Whitehead, *Religion in the Making* (New York: Fordham University Press, 1996), p. 74. This statement echoes Rousseau's claim (*The Social Contract*, book 4, ch. 8) that 'Christianity preaches nothing but servitude and dependence. Its spirit is so favourable to tyranny that tyranny always profits from it.'

make the mission more than simply the externalization required in order to spread the message of salvation; it would then also be the form in which the church, opposed to the 'world', worked through its irresolvable conflict with that 'world'. The corresponding formula should be: going on the offensive by fleeing from the world – or, to put it more mildly: serving the world from a position of scepticism towards the world.

One can assess how far these somewhat uneasy suppositions are justified with reference to the effects of the church teacher Aurelius Augustinus. He can claim the privilege of having contributed more than any other individual believer – except Paul – to the confusion, and in fact the neuroticization, of a civilization. This diagnosis by no means refers only to the sexual-pathological distortions that were forced on Christian forms of life for one and a half centuries. The metaphysics of predestination taught by Augustine was even more harmful: upon closer inspection, it reveals itself as the most unfathomable system of terror in the history of religion.[12] As the doctrine of the eternal predestination of Adam's children was based on an axiom stating that only very few would undeservedly be saved, while the majority would deservedly be cast into the flames, weighed down by the 'burden of damnation', the edifice of Christian faith after Augustine could only be erected over the tormenting uncertainty of one's own predetermined salvation. The only vague indication for individuals of possibly being chosen came from the fact that, with God's help, they could progress from fearful trembling to zealotry. It is no coincidence, then, that with Augustine – following preludes in the deserts of the Near East – the flight of believers to the monastic

---

[12] *Logik des Schreckens* [The Logic of Terror]. *Augustinus von Hippo: De diversis quaestiones ad Simplicianum I, 2. Die Gnadenlehre von 397* [The Doctrine of Grace from 397], trans. Walter Schäfer, and edited with notes and an afterword by Kurt Flasch (Mainz: Dieterich'sche Verlagsbuchhandlung, 1990), Latin–German.

orders in late antiquity also began in the Western sphere; these orders offered a liveable form for the total absorption of being through the religious imperative. Yet even if Augustinism declared complete subservience to the gospel as the precondition for salvation – a compacted anticipation of Islam – neither resolute zealotry nor strict self-renunciation could guarantee the salvation of the individual. Conversely, the slightest trace of indifference to the good news could be read as an almost certain indication of predestination to damnation.

Whoever desires to trace the underlying modus operandi of Augustinian Christianity with analytical clarity will find it, brilliantly disguised by the winning discourse of God's all-encompassing love, in the devious and systematic combination of a rational universalism of damnation and an unfathomable elitism of salvation. In order to do the theologian's doctrine greater justice, it may be useful to realize the ways in which all great religions have a part in a general economy of cruelty. Its application lies in ostensibly lowering the general level of cruelty by inducing believers to take a certain amount of suffering upon themselves voluntarily in order to avoid or hold back greater unwanted terrors. This forms the basis for the transformative effects of spiritual asceticisms. One of the most attractive aspects of early Christianity was its dissolution of the standards of the Roman culture of cruelty – especially through its resistance to the brutalizing gladiatorial games, which had developed into a ubiquitous form of decadent mass culture in the Roman Empire (comparable only to the perversions of top-level sports in the second half of the twentieth century). Augustine intensified this resistance by striving for a moderation of human behaviour through the threat of maximum cruelty in the life beyond. With this approach, however, he fell prey to the danger of overshooting the mark: with his unflinching theological absolutism, this most influential of all the church fathers inflated the diabolical aspect of God to the point of sacred terrorism. It can therefore be said that Augustinian Christianity proved a victim of fatal losses: because metaphysical terror inevitably translates into psychological, and ultimately also physical, terror, Augustine's ungracious doctrine of grace contributed to raising the level of cruelty in the Christianized world through the gospel, rather than lowering it. In this sense, Christianity's critics touch on a raw nerve when they argue that Christianity often furthered the evil from which it subsequently offered deliverance.

Considering all this, one can understand why countless Christians have only been able to adopt Augustine's doctrines by repressing their unpalatable aspects. The history of the Christian faith since the early Middle Ages is nothing but a series of attempts to mask the sinister dimensions of the Augustinian legacy through a more optimistic interpretation of the question of humanity's chances of salvation. Hardly any Christian ever had the necessary cold-bloodedness to realize why heaven had to remain almost empty – as far as human dwellers were concerned, at least – during the era dominated by Augustine's theology. It was only with the age of discoveries that believers were presented with the task of exploring the practically untouched continent of divine generosity. From that point on, the aim was to depict the realm of God beyond this world as a densely populated area – Dante would have been one of the first to encounter more than a ghost town on his journey to heaven. The current results of the search for a generous God were expressed in the Polish pope's well-known statement: *speriamo che l'inferno sia vuoto* – 'let us hope that hell is empty'. The antithesis between Augustine and John Paul II encapsulates the whole drama of Christian theology: it shows the long way from the well-guarded terrorist secret of faith, in which God remained virtually alone in heaven, to the civil-religiously tinged hypothesis by which hell – in which one is still supposed to believe owing to the fact of our 'distance from God' – should remain empty in future.

The question of whether the full blame for the darkening influence of Augustinian doctrines on Christianity should be laid upon their originator will be left open here. In his way, he was the medium of a bad time that made superhuman demands on his brilliance; it is hardly surprising that this resulted in some inhumane solutions. It is only regrettable that the fifth century did not produce any author with sufficient understanding to formulate the thesis: whoever did not live before Augustine knows nothing of life's sweetness. *Douceur de vivre*, however, is a concept that could only become meaningful again once one had reached the safe shore of post-Augustinian, in a way even post-Christian (in the sense of post-clericocratic), times. This marked the start of an age in which popes would feel obliged to point out that Christianity should not revolve primarily around compulsion and self-denial, but rather a positive way of life.

On the whole, Christianity's campaign to conquer the 'globe' owes its success to its episcopal guidance, which sought a balance between eschatological extremism and magical populism in the course of a learning process that continued for centuries. During its first expansion cycle, the secret of the Christian missions' success lay primarily in its alliances with political rulers and a specific strategy of converting nobles – the Constantinian shift provided the most brilliant and most questionable model for this. Whoever was interested in spreading Christianity in the age of monarchy had to follow the maxim that one can only win over the people if one has the local ruler on one's side.

As far as the infamous crusades or the Holy War are concerned, these are of secondary significance compared to the proselytistic or missionary mode of expansion – if, that is, one wishes to credit them with any genuine offensive significance at all. Certainly the crusade, as the prototype of a war inspired by Christianity, unleashed enormous resources and is often believed by internal and external critics alike to exemplify the religion's inherent aggression. A single glance at the historical connections, however, shows that the (conventionally counted) seven major ventures of this kind between 1096 and 1270 were, from the crusaders' point of view, primarily measures to contain the Islamic offensive – and their lack of success underlines the relative accuracy of this judgement. They were intended to take over what Christians viewed as the centre of the world – Jerusalem – or protect it from a supposedly inappropriate occupation, but not to open the entire world to Christianity by force. The claim one occasionally hears that the crusades to Jerusalem caused the deaths of more than 20 million people seems itself to be zealous in its exaggeration.

The most favourable account of the 'armed pilgrimages' to the Holy Land was probably penned by Hegel, who saw them as an indispensable experience for the curriculum of the spirit. In dialectics, experience is synonymous with productive disappointment, in so far as it reverses consciousness and enlightens it as to the falsity of its still badly abstract preconceptions. Hegel argues that, by seeking to force the holy and subtle by profane and crude means, the crusaders 'combined opposing elements without any reconciliation' in their battles; hence their failure was in the nature of the enterprise. The only lasting value lay in the realization of how misguided it is to seek the Highest in such an external form – here one can discern firstly the enlightened Protestant critique of the love of fetishes in Catholic populism, and secondly the speculative philosopher's declaration of war on the mechanics of 'positive religion'. It is fitting, then, that the crusade as a behavioural pattern had a purely metaphorical meaning from the Modern Age onwards. General Eisenhower was able to publish his memoirs from the Second World War in 1948 under the – to Anglophone ears – entirely conventional title *Crusade in Europe* without anyone suspecting an underlying Christian agenda.

In previous centuries, on the other hand, there had been no lack of compulsive Christianizing enterprises that directly combined a war of aggression with mission, for example in Charlemagne's Saxon Wars or the conquest of Prussia and the Baltic by the Teutonic Knights. With Christianity acting as the imperial religion and state cult, the imposition of church uniforms was the order of the day. In addition, such factors as the maintenance of Latin as the church language, Thomism and canonical law played a part in enforcing Roman Catholic standards with sublimely compulsive homogeneity.

Christianity's most powerful expansionist campaigns took place during the post-medieval period. What we now call globalization, or rather its terrestrial phase,[13] is inseparable from the paradoxical path of Christianity into the openness of modernity. From the sixteenth century on, Rome launched a second apostolic wave with the founding of missionary orders, initiating the operative universalization of religion in the form of Christianity. In practice, the world mission usually acted as a partner and parasite of colonialism, and only rarely as its critic or opponent.[14] Ironically, the Roman Catholic world missions, which were accompanied belatedly, but successfully, by the Protestant enterprises, reached the zenith of their effectiveness from the eighteenth century onwards, the century that marked the start of Europe's dechristianization – or, to put it more cautiously, the start of religion's differentiation into a subsystem of its own. And, while the nineteenth century was characterized in the Old World by anti-Christian offensives that looked down on Christianity like a vanquished formation after their rise to cultural hegemony, that same epoch must, in mission-historical terms, be viewed as the golden age of external Christianization. Only now did the spreading of Christian missions

---

[13] Peter Sloterdijk, *Im Weltinnenraum des Kapitals. Für eine philosophische Theorie der Globalisierung* [In the World Interior of Capital. For a Philosophical Theory of Globalization] (Frankfurt am Main: Suhrkamp, 2006).

[14] Horst Gründer, *Welteroberung und Christentum. Ein Handbuch zur Geschichte der Neuzeit* [World Conquest and Christianity. A Handbook for the History of the Modern Age] (Gütersloh, 1992).

across the entire globe and the founding of sustainable church communities in the remotest corners of the world become a practical reality.[15] Since then, Christianity has been the leading world religion in numerical terms, not least because of the incorporation of the populous continent of South America into the remotely controlled Roman Catholic empire.

The second irony of dechristianization is evident in the fact that the new major cultural force in Europe, the Enlightenment, amounted to a continuation of Christianity by rationalist and historico-philosophical means by virtue of its ideological or propagandistic design. It has been plausibly argued that the moral core of the Enlightenment, the doctrine of human rights, can only be explained as the secularized version of Christian anthropology. (I will speak further below about the formation of a fourth wave that flooded modern 'society' as a 'human' monotheism.) It is no coincidence that the adherents of Protestantism and Catholicism are now quarrelling over the royalties for human rights. The continuities become most vivid if one considers the adoption of Christian monotheistic models by the zealots of secular modernity. This applies in particular to the human-churchly fanaticism of the Jacobins. But the militantism of Lenin's professional revolutionaries or even the fury of the Red Guards in Mao Zedong's China contain elements of a continuation of Christian universalism by un-Christian means. They can only be fully understood as feral imitations of the apostolic modus vivendi. As unbelievable as it may sound, even the Chinese students who humiliated, beat and murdered their professors during the Cultural Revolution from 1966 onwards believed they were ambassadors of a just cause and acting for the good of all. Had that not been the case, it would not have been possible

---

[15] Ernst Benz, *Beschreibung des Christentums. Eine historische Phänomenologie* [Description of Christianity. A Historical Phenomenology] (Munich, 1975), pp. 29 and 302.

for parts of the Western European intelligentsia to be affected by a collective Maoist psychosis during the 1960s and 1970s – still one of the darkest chapters of recent intellectual history. The members of these circles heard the signature melody of unfettered egalitarianism in the Chinese excesses, a melody that had first sounded in Europe during the Jacobin terror and has since been used as a carrier for all manner of texts around the world. In the light of these phenomena, it is not without a certain anxiety that one recalls Leo Baeck's sublimely naïve thesis that the future is essentially the future of good, a future to which all coming days will lead.[16]

Studying the frenzy in China – which consisted of rather more than a few regrettable incidents, as forgetful ex-Maoists in France and elsewhere like to suggest – can provide insight into the dangerous nature of universalist militants: for example, how quickly uncontrolled universalism can lead to a fascism of the good. It remains uncontrolled if it lacks a critical organ to restrain the zealots' urge to absolutize their goals. With this stance, the activist is neither willing nor able to attain the insight on which any enlightened political morality is based, namely that it is not the end that justifies the means, but rather the means that tell us the truth about the ends. As we know, the direst forms of terror are those motivated by the loftiest of intentions. More than a few of those possessed by the demon of goodness genuinely told themselves that crimes can be the highest form of divine service or fulfilment of the duty to humanity. The most effective objection to such enchantments comes from the spiritual core of the Christian religion: from the perspective of paying attention to the means, Jesus' theorem 'you shall know them by their fruits' (Matthew 7:16) and Marshall McLuhan's crypto-Christological maxim 'the medium is the message' mean the same thing.

---

[16] Baeck, *Das Wesen des Judentums*, p. 266. Also ibid., p. 261: 'The true history of the world is the history of good.'

From a synoptic point of view, one should note that Christianity's campaigns, especially after the severe setbacks encountered during the Age of Enlightenment, only seem capable of continuation in a somewhat more muted fashion. After its worldwide expansionist successes, which resulted in roughly one-third of the planet's population living under its influence, without all of these even being conscious or active Christians, one would hardly expect any further spread – unless the intense dynamic of secular reform and its spiritual lacunae in East Asia, particularly China, result in the growth of a new religious market. Thus one can summarize the provisional endpoint of the Christian campaign with the observation that this religion today combines a relative maximum of dissemination with a relative minimum of intensity. Its condition proves that there can be not only imperial, but also simultaneous spiritual, 'overstretching'.

With increasing success comes increasing entropy. Under its influence, the universalist potential of faith is confirmed and simultaneously pensioned off by the great church organizations. Entropic phenomena are also unmistakably responsible for the changing face of faith in the USA, where, as Harold Bloom incisively observed, the last fifty years have seen a reshaping of Protestant Christianity into a post-Christian 'American religion' with pronounced gnostic, individualistic and Machiavellist aspects.[17] Here, the faith in the Father has almost entirely disappeared, while the narcissistic realm of the Son no longer tolerates resistance. If there were an American trinity it would consist of Jesus, Machiavelli and the spirit of money. The postmodern credo was formulated in exemplary fashion by the Afro-American actor Forest Whitaker when he gave his speech of thanks upon receiving the Oscar for the best leading role in 2007, closing with the words: 'And I thank God for always believing in me.'

---

[17] Harold Bloom, *The American Religion: The Emergence of the Post-Christian Nation* (New York: Simon & Schuster, 1992), p. 184.

The intentional universalism of Christianity, however, was inevitably foiled in the twentieth century by the pragmatic necessities arising from coexistence with other creeds – and the charitable weakening of the churches through the development of self-confidently secular forms of life. The Christian confessions attended the school of pluralism and became predictable factors in the world ecumenical movement. From this perspective, Christianity, at least with regard to its broad central field, has entered its 'post-imperial' period, and – as far as one can tell – irreversibly so. The radical sects are an exception to this, especially at the evangelical end of the spectrum: they 'use fundamentalism as a means of re-universalization'.[18] One can profit from them as unwitting enlighteners by listening to them as informants on the universalism of the lunatics. This is not, however, the place to discuss – let alone decide – whether one should take their example as representative of the hysterical nature of all militant universalism.

Finally, I would like to turn to the question of whether Islam too is committed to its own specific campaign. The obvious answer would seem to be in the affirmative, but any more precise elaboration comes up against various obstacles for fundamental and historical reasons. The historical complications result from the fact that, after an initial phase of rapid expansion and great imperial prosperity, the Islamic world, whose fate was initially identical to that of the Arab sphere as a whole, fell into a long period of stagnation and regression whose possible end only became foreseeable with the demographic explosiveness and fundamentalist reform dynamic of

---

[18] Cf. Olivier Roy, *Globalised Islam: Fundamentalism, De-territorialisation and the Search for a New Ummah* (London: C. Hurst & Co., 2004), p. 331: 'Fundamentalism is a means of re-universalising religions (whether it be Islam or Christianity) that has ended up being closely identified with a given culture.'

the twentieth century. As far as the difficulties of a fundamental nature are concerned, these are combined above all with the contentious interpretation of the term *jihad*, whose appropriation by radical Islamic terrorist sects in recent times continues to spawn polemics and counter-statements.

A first indication of the inherent offensive dynamic of Islamic preaching can be gained through the observation that the earliest suras, which followed the divine revelations of 610 and the years immediately after it (such as the famous Meccan sura 81 *al-Takwirk*, The Folding Up), predominantly follow the tunes of apocalyptic escalation, the final decision and the threat of the terrors of Judgement Day.[19] The tendency of the other early suras is one of an unconditional separation from conventional religious practices in Mecca and elsewhere: 'Say to them: you unbelievers! I do not honour what you honour, and you do not honour what I honour' (Sura 109:1f.). It is equally evident that the starting point of the Islamic commune as a small, sworn community did not constitute an ideal, but was intended to be overcome as quickly as possible. Furthermore, the first *ummah* of Medina that gathered around the prophet was anything but a contemplative idyll. Its chronicle tells of numerous martial confrontations, starting with the ominous skirmish at the waterhole of Badr. It deals with the prophet's controversial caravan raids, shifting strategic alliances, an attack on the palm grove of a rival party that was scandalous for Arabs, and the casual massacre of a Jewish minority. But whatever religious meanings might be read into these episodes, they already give clear indications of what was to follow. The imperative of growth was no less intrinsic to this religious foundation than it was to Paul's mission – with the difference

---

[19] Annemarie Schimmel, *Die Religion des Islam. Eine Einführung* [The Religion of Islam: An Introduction] (Stuttgart: Reclaim, 1990), pp. 14f.

that the political–military and religious dynamics here formed an inseparable a-priori unity. Mohammed followed on from the escalation of post-Babylonian Judaism, which lived on in the zealotic escalation of Paul, developing these elements further to form an integral militantism. He achieved this by making – like an Arab Paul – the apostolic form of life, the self-consumption in the proclamation and the proclaimed, binding for all the members of his commune. In this way, the maximum religious existence, the complete devotion to God's instructions, was declared a standard expectation of all people – in fact, almost the bare minimum of service to the Almighty that humans should carry out. That is why the word *islām*, which literally means 'submission', also gave the religion its name.

The binding nature of this guiding concept for all Muslims has foreseeable consequences: it transfers the prophet's zealotry normatively to his followers' way of life – and inversely to the fates of the unbelievers. The constitutive role of the martial factor is reinforced by the fact that the canonic writings on the prophet include a subgroup, known as the *maghazi* literature, that deals exclusively with Mohammed's military campaigns; in them one finds a normative inflation of sacred militantism. This final escalation finds its most vivid expression in the compulsory prayer (*salāt*) to be carried out 5 times per day, each time with 17 bows and 2 prostrations. Thus every practising Muslim performs 85 bows to Allah and 10 prostrations daily, making 29,090 bows and 3,540 prostrations per lunar year, as well as the corresponding recitations. In Christianity, such intensive rehearsal is only demanded within monastic orders, with a daily quota of seven hours of prayer. Logically enough, the Arabic word for 'mosque', *masjid*, means 'place of prostration'. One should not underestimate the formative effect of frequent ritual actions. The prophet says so himself: *Ad-dînu mu'amala* – 'religion is behaviour'. This is why some Islamic scholars are right in going so far as to claim that ritual prayer is a form of jihad.[20] That may sound effusive, but it describes a psychosemantically evident reality. What goes on in Muslim houses of prayer thus serves not only the manifestation of faith. The relationship with transcendence celebrated physically and psychologically on a daily basis becomes equally effective as a way of keeping in shape for projects of holy dispute. From an ethical and pragmatic perspective, Islam succeeded in absorbing zealotry completely into daily life through the universal duty of ritual prayer. The greatest of all duties is memoactive fitness: it equals the spirit of the law itself.

Given the familiarity of the subject, I will be permitted to refrain from recounting the astounding history of Islamic expansion leading to the foundation of the various caliphates under the Umayyads, the Abbasids, the Fatimids, the Ottomans, etc. The explosive spread of Islam in the one-and-a-half centuries following the prophet's death is undeniably one of the political-military wonders of the world, surpassed only by the extensively and intensively even more significant expansion of the British Empire between the sixteenth and nineteenth centuries. It cannot be doubted for a moment that this rapid, albeit regionally limited, world conquest was based on the most authentic intentions of Islam and its holy scriptures. What some have referred to as 'the venture of Islam'[21] was founded on a vigorous ethic of expansion. Never was this more successful than in the time of the early caliphs; all practical realizations of Islam-specific dreams of a world empire originate from them.[22] The frequently read claim that the

---

[20] Seyyed Hossein Nasr, 'The Spiritual Significance of Jihad' in *Traditional Islam in the Modern World*, ed. Nasr (London: Kegan Paul, 1987).
[21] Marshall G. S. Hodgson, *The Venture of Islam. Conscience and History in a World Civilization*, vols. I-III (Chicago: University of Chicago Press, 1974).
[22] Efraim Karsh, *Islamic Imperialism: A History* (New Haven: Yale University Press, 2007).

Arab conquests were of a purely political nature, that forced conversions of the conquered only took place very rarely, and certainly not with people of the book – because Islam rejects the use of force in religious matters – is a well-meaning protective statement whose true core lies beneath a thick shell of contradictory facts. Otherwise it would be inexplicable why, following the Arabian peninsula, such countries as Syria, Palestine, Mesopotamia, Egypt, Libya, Morocco and Spain, but also large parts of Anatolia, Iran, the Caucasus and North India were taken up, with lasting or at least long-term consequences, into the Islamic religious space. Here one can apply Rousseau's theory that in earlier times, 'since there was no means of converting people except by subduing them, the only missionaries were conquerors'.[23] Certainly some people would have embraced the Islamic faith because of their own inclination and conviction, but it can hardly be denied that, for most new believers, conversion began with an armed invitation to prayer. Later generations found Islam as the ruling religion, experiencing it as a fact of culture that one acquires through the mild tyranny of education. What began with devout conventions came to fruition through the internalization of the memoactive stigma.

The history of the campaign of Islam can, despite regional setbacks and schisms verging on civil war, be related as a consistent success story until the fifteenth century AD (the ninth century by the Muslim calendar). Up to that point, the supremacy of Arab and Islamic civilization was incontestable in most areas, starting with their superior military power. In its golden age, Islam was also the most important economic force in the world, as can be seen from the intercontinental connections it cultivated. Its colourful bazaars were legendary, and the variety of the selection at its slave markets was unparalleled. Furthermore, Islamic scientists and artists

---

[23] Jean-Jacques Rousseau, *The Social Contract*, trans. Maurice Cranston (London: Penguin Books, 1968), p. 178.

embodied the highest level of achievement up to the turn of the thirteenth century. The assimilative power of Islamic culture for knowledge and skills from other parts of the world seemed to know no boundaries – until the bigoted reactionary movements in the thirteenth century (not forgetting the disastrous effects of the Mongol attack of 1258) brought this high-cultural splendour to an end.[24] Nonetheless, it took centuries for the heirs of the Islamic heyday to notice the stagnation. When Constantinople was conquered by Ottoman troops in 1453, there was a general conviction that Christian Europe was now also ripe for conquest.

In their seemingly well-founded sense of superiority, most members of the Islamic cultural realm had missed the fact that they were in the process of being outdone by the 'miserable infidels' of the north-west – in the fields of theology, philosophy and worldly science from the thirteenth century on; in the visual arts from the fourteenth and fifteenth centuries on; as well as economically from the fifteenth and sixteenth centuries on, which was due particularly to the superior European seafaring and the transition to modern property economy alias capitalism, with its dynamic of constant innovation. The achievements of the distant enemy could seemingly be ignored with impunity as long as people were living under the protection of timeless revelations and sublime governments. They were not able or willing to see that they had locked themselves in the prison of tradition. Finally, in the eighteenth century, the military supremacy of the Europeans was made shockingly clear – the trauma of Napoleon's Egyptian expedition in 1798 is still acute more than two centuries later. From the moment that Europe's ascent to global dominance could no longer be overlooked,

---

[24] A later symbol of triumphant bigotry is the destruction of the observatory in Istanbul, built in 1577 on the initiative of the mathematician and astronomer Taküyiddin Efendi, by the sultan's naval artillery in 1580.

the proud chronicle of Islam's campaigns turned into a never-ending history of insult. The disappointment of those left behind grew into bitterness from the eighteenth century on, and the noisy European expansionism of the nineteenth century was hardly likely to mitigate this sentiment. Since then, the extremely thymotic culture of the Islamic countries has been cloaked in a veil of anger woven from the conflicting sentiments of a longing for splendour and dominance on the one hand and a chronic feeling of resentment on the other. From that point on, pride in the past was always accompanied by a scarcely concealable shame at the current state of affairs.

Characteristically, the growth of a new zealotry in Islam can be traced back to the eighteenth century, when even the most introverted Muslims could no longer overlook the exhausted state of both their culture and their religion. Wahabbism, which sought redemption in a return to a literal interpretation of the Qur'an, was typical of the reactionary tendencies of the time, while in the nineteenth century the most characteristic movement was Salafism, which can best be understood as an ascetic romanticism and whose followers dreamed of the early *ummah* and the righteous predecessors (*salaf as-salih*) of Medina. Since the middle of the eighteenth century, then, a temptation had been in the air to alleviate the plight of Islam in the age of confrontation with the superior West through zealotic escalation and restorative collectives. By claiming more adamantly than ever to be under the just guidance of Allah, the new zealots resolutely chose not to learn from the enemy – and thus likewise to ignore the voices of the present. Perhaps they thought that bowing to God's authority entitled them to oppose the authority of the rest of the world. The Arabocentrism of these reactions was a further factor in weakening the Islamic world, as it encouraged the tendency to ignore the internal diversity of the Muslim universe, as exemplified by the spiritual and cultural treasures of the Persian-Shiite and Turkish-Ottoman epicentres. The consequences of this choice proved disastrous for the entire Islamic hemisphere, as they reinforced the tendency towards defiant intractability in the face of the demands made by an age of new openings. Viewing oneself as a victim of foreign powers became a widespread approach, and when victims come together with other victims, it does not take long for culprits to be named. Bernard Lewis describes the harmful effects of these reactionary tendencies. It is only with great delay and in tentative forms that people in the Middle East are becoming willing to examine their own behaviour: 'The question "Who did this to us?" has led only to neurotic fantasies and conspiracy theories. The other question – "What did we do wrong?" – has led naturally to a second question: "How do we put it right?" In that question, and in the various answers that are being found, lie the best hopes for the future.'[25]

The campaign-like qualities of the 'venture of Islam' can thus, as we have seen, be established historically with somewhat clear contours. They also, however, invite an evaluation at a fundamental level in so far as they are connected closely to orthodox and orthopractically lived religion. This is where the meanwhile infamous concept of jihad comes into view, that 'striving on the path of God' through which Islam seeks to train its believers, generally without exception, as zealots for the kingdom of God. This tradition makes militantism a part of Muslim life from the outset, and the only reason it is not officially included among the famous five 'pillars' of Islam is that it is implicitly understood in all of them. Islam therefore constitutes not only the most pronounced final form of offensive religious universalism (rivalled only, temporarily, by Communism); its design practically makes it a religion of encampments. Permanent movement is inher-

---

[25] Bernard Lewis, *What Went Wrong? Western Impact and Middle Eastern Response* (Oxford: Oxford University Press, 2002), p. 159. Lewis attributes Turkey's path towards modernity to Atatürk's constructive answers to the second question.

ent in it – and any stasis must be viewed with suspicion as the beginning of a falling away from faith. In this respect Mohammed faithfully followed Paul's model, with the significant difference that the latter, as a civilian and Roman citizen, preferred peaceful zealotry. Islamic zealotry has always had an element of martial devotion, underpinned by a richly embellished mysticism of martyrdom. It would be an exaggeration to describe the aggressive mujaheddin of the Caliphate as professional revolutionaries of God, but their willingness to use force for the noble cause certainly increases the similarities. The contemporary Egyptian author Sa'id Ayyub postulates the God-given duty for Muslims to shed their blood in the Holy War against the anti-Muslim Satan: 'That is our destiny, from the battle of Badr (in 624) to the day of the antichrist.'[26]

It may be that the internalization of jihad taught from the twelfth century on, following the efforts of the Sufi mystic Al Ghazali, bore fine fruits in the peace of the Islamic rear lines. But the fact that one could describe the inner battle as the major jihad and the external battle as the minor only proves that even Islam, normally known for its sobriety, was not immune to excessive enthusiasm. The popularization of jihad in the conflicts of the present results in the desublimation of the concept and thus the return to its first meaning, regardless of all objections from spiritual exegetes. The idea of a battle against the base self gave rise to a conceptualized militantism without any external enemy, as one can also observe in the reshaping of the Far Eastern art of war into spiritualized fighting disciplines. The subtle jihad needed to be waged as a campaign against the heathen residue within one's own soul – with the believer discovering rebellious oases and anarchic provinces within himself that have not yet been reached by the dominion of the law. With the return of

---

[26] Quoted from David Cook, *Contemporary Muslim Apocalyptic Literature* (Syracuse: Syracuse University Press, 2005), p. 210.

the real enemy, even if only on the level of misunderstandings and projections, the metaphorical meanings disappear. These are replaced once more by concrete acts of war against physical opponents both near and distant. The modern agitators say it loudly and clearly: the believer should not sleep as long as he is living within a non-Islamic political system; his life can only take on meaning if it is devoted to the abolition of foreign dominance.[27] Those who fall in this battle have secured their place in paradise; unbelievers who die in the unjust battle against Muslims, on the other hand, go directly to hell. Although they have no scholarly authority, the activists in the militant organizations of today know which suras to refer to. Their actions may be appalling, but their quotations are perfect.

All commentaries on Islamic neo-expansionism in the late twentieth and early twenty-first centuries would remain idle speculation had Islam, as a religion and a cultural model, not been bolstered by two recent developments that have, within a short time, made it politically significant once again. The first of these changes is of an economic-technological nature, the second of a biopolitical one. Firstly, a number of states under Islamic rule – more specifically, the upper classes of such countries as Saudi Arabia, Iran and Iraq, and to a lesser extent also Libya and Egypt – have profited both economically and politically from the fact that up to 60 per cent of the world's oil reserves either have been found or are believed to be located within their borders. In the age of fossil fuels, this situation has, despite the well-known inefficiency of their governments, the often-criticized backwardness of their social structures and the insecurity of their legal systems, provided the oil-producing countries of the Middle East with the resources to live far beyond

---

[27] Sayyid Abdul A'la Mawdudi, *The Islamic Way of Life* (Leicester: The Islamic Foundation, 1986).

their means. The second tendency reinforces this dubious economic situation. Between 1900 and 2000, the population of the Islamic hemisphere has increased from roughly 150 million to 1.2 billion people, eight times as many – a dynamic of increase that is unprecedented, even with the broadest historical view. One part of this explosion can be attributed to conditions that support a reproduction of poverty, while another part is culturally and religiously determined, as an abundance of children is still valued highly by conservative Muslims; a further part can probably be attributed to a more or less conscious policy of militant reproduction, as there have long been numerous ideologues in Islamic countries who are proud to carry the 'banner of reproduction'. These factors shape the conditions under which the resumption of offensively universalist programmes by elements of militant Islamism could become the order of the day. The frequent fantasies in militant circles of re-establishing the world caliphate also show, admittedly, that more than a few radicals live in isolated alternative realities. For them, the surrealism that lies in all religions grows into a reverie with open eyes. They work on a purely imaginary agenda that can no longer be reconciled with any actual history. The only link between their constructs and the rest of the world is the terrorist attack with as many dead as possible, whose scenic form corresponds to a raid from the dream world into reality.

To summarize, one cannot reach any definite judgement on the campaign of Islam in its fifteenth century. The chances of a further expansion of its external mission can only be viewed with reserve – even if Europe's current vulnerability dictates certain fear scenarios. Its current successes are, as far as one can tell, restricted primarily to underprivileged classes in European and African societies – and, when they do involve the educated, to the descendants of immigrants from Islamic countries who have returned to their original religion after a period of estrangement. Its main motor is the growing radicalization of its own rampant excess of young men.[28] Islam seems to be rather less attractive to the elites of Asia, America and Europe. Statistics show that conversions to Islam increase at times when this religion comes under greater criticism – which points to the psychodynamics of an identification with a threatened cause. In the longer term, the poor organization and disunity of the Islamic states and associations make successful political expansion unlikely. Even if there were such results, no one would know how to make use of them in the sense of any centralized planning. If Islam reached the same number of followers as Christianity by the end of the twenty-first century, which statisticians and strategists by no means consider impossible, this would be due almost entirely to its self-cultivated population growth, and only to a very small degree to its spiritual aura. As far as the religious authority of Islam in its two main movements is concerned, it is increasingly being crushed by the implosion of hierarchies and the dissolution of the traditional order of knowledge.[29] Furthermore, it has been damaged so heavily by the almost automatic association between Islamism and terror in the world's consciousness that it is difficult to imagine how Islam in its totality, as a religion and a matrix of cultures, could recover from this in the foreseeable future. At any rate, the 'house of Islam' will be faced with modernization crises of frightening intensity. It has transformed itself into the 'house of war', which Muslims traditionally liked to believe pointed to the extra-Islamic dimensions of the world.[30] Perhaps educated Europeans living around the year 2050, observing the chronic convulsions of

---

[28] Gunnar Heinsohn, *Söhne und Weltmacht. Terror im Aufstieg und Fall der Nationen* [Sons and World Power. Terror in the Rise and Fall of Nations], 4th edition (Zurich, 2006).
[29] Cf. Roy, *Globalised Islam: Fundamentalism, De-territorialisation and the Search for a New Ummah.*
[30] Gilles Kepel, *The War for Muslim Minds: Islam and the West*, trans. Pascale Ghazaleh (Cambridge, Mass.: Belknap Press, 2006).

Islamic 'societies', will occasionally be reminded of the battles of the reformation age – but even more strongly of Catholicism's anti-modern phase of defiance, which lasted from 1789 until the Second Vatican Council and which, one is still amazed to recall, ended to the advantage of all concerned with a reconciliation of theocentrism and democracy.

5

The matrix

What has so far been said about the formations, fronts and campaigns of the three monotheisms demands integration within an overview of the logical patterns of the faith in one god and the blueprints for zealous universalisms. It would be misleading to assume that monotheistic zeal is a matter determined first and foremost by emotional laws and therefore calls primarily for a psychological analysis. Naturally the affect-dynamic aspects of zealotry are open to psychosemantic probing. It would be reckless to ignore the depth-psychological insights into religio-neurotic and clericopathic phenomena gathered in the course of the nineteenth and twentieth centuries – to name only the well-studied examples of God's helper syndrome and spiritual masochism. Psychoanalysis also specialized in revealing the parallels between individual people's images of God and their images of their parents. Furthermore, such authors as Kierkegaard, Dostoyevsky, Nietzsche, Heidegger and others showed that what is generally presented as faith is often a form of hysteria – an act whose protagonists muster their entire existences in the hope of gaining desired roles at the religious vanity fair. Where there is zeal, there is competitive zeal, and what initially seems to be an intimate affair between God and the soul is not infrequently also fuelled by the jealousy of ambitious souls regarding the real and imagined advantages of their rivals in the battle for the best seats.

On the other hand, more recent religio-psychological research – supported by new hybrid subjects like neuro-theology and neuro-rhetoric[1] – has given indications of the 'biopositive' effects of religious affects that, if one is to avoid a one-sided view, cannot be ignored. With all due respect for the findings in the fields of psychological and biological research, the monotheism of the exclusive and totalitarian type under debate here contains one primary logical problem for us to decipher, and this problem follows its own strictly internally conditioned grammar. One of the points of departure in gaining an understanding of the laws that determine the construction of the exclusive monotheisms has already been touched on in the references to Abraham's quest for a god worthy of his adoration. The typical summotheistic climb to the final, the highest and the utmost contains the logical implication that one must move from the plural to the singular, from the many gods to the one God. A deity that was the Highest but not the One would be inconceivable at this level of reflection. Religious supremacism, the ascent to the Highest and the Only, is necessarily tied to ontological monarchism – the principle that a single being can and should rule over everyone and everything.[2] This monarchism is joined by a dynamism which ensures that nothing can resist the overlord, in keeping with the theorem *omnia apud deum facilia* – 'naturally everything is easy for God'. From this dynamism follows optimism (or perfectionism, to put it more precisely in idea-historical terms), which states that the dominant one is the perfect

---

[1] For critical positions, cf. Detlev B. Linke, *Religion als Risiko. Geist, Glaube und Gehirn* [Religion As Risk. Spirit, Faith and the Brain] (Reinbek: Rowohlt, 2003); Hamer, *The God Gene: How Faith Is Hardwired into Our Genes*; Andrew Newberg, Eugene D'Aquili and Vince Rause, *Why God Won't Go Away: Brain Science and the Biology of Belief* (New York: Ballantine Books, 2001); Mühlmann, *Jesus überlistet Darwin.*
[2] Erik Peterson, *Theologische Traktate* [Theological Treatises] (Munich: Kösel-Verlag, 1951).

and the best, and always acts in accordance with his perfect nature. The best is the one who is better than everything good – or more than that: better than everything that is merely better than good.

This supremacist thought climbs numerous steps to reach the peak of the hyper-best, which ultimately subjugates all things and beings both *de facto* and *de jure*. It culminates in a figure known in the language of faith as God, the eternal and almighty. It is to him and only to him that the rule applies: the elevation to the Highest must consistently follow the trail of a personal transcendence. In this scheme, God alone can be placed as a person above all other persons, as the author, the creator, the lawmaker, the ruler and the director of the world's theatre, the one without whose command not a single hair falls from a human head – and without whose support no household appliance works.[3] A conspicuous feature of this God is a strong preponderance of *you* qualities – accompanied by underdeveloped *id* elements. His invitation is more to a relationship than to insight. Once the believer, like Dostoyevsky's Prince Myshkin, has become wholly childlike and wholly idiotic in relation to the almighty other, the last traces of God's cognitive determinacy dissolve.

As long as we are dealing with Abrahamites, then, we are operating within the sphere of the subjective highest, whose condensate appears in the idea of a transcendent kingship. This is expressed as much in the Jewish idea of the theocracy of Yahweh as in the doctrine of Christ's royal reign (see the encyclical *Quas primas* published by Pius XI in 1925) and the idea, ubiquitous in Islam, of Allah's omnipotence, which is supposed to apply in both the political and everyday pragmatic spheres.[4] The monarch of personal supremacism is not only the creator,

---

[3] Cf. Luhmann, *Die Religion der Gesellschaft*, p. 160.
[4] A late example of monotheistic symbolism was provided in December 2006 by the forty-six 'conservative' members of the Polish parliament who applied for Christ to be declared King of Poland.

ruler and preserver of the world, but also its archivist, saviour, judge and – *in extremis* – its avenger and destroyer.

It is easy to understand now why the relationship between humans and a highest being of the personal type is subject to completely different laws from those in the case of an impersonal supreme power. It is part and parcel of this form of personal supremacism that those who think and believe cannot be any more than mere vassals or employees of the divine sovereign – the only other option being the despicable role of infidels and disobedients. Whether they like it or not, the supremacization of the personal God inevitably assigns humans an inferior status. The most important asymmetry between servant and master manifests itself in the fact that God remains unfathomable to humans, even once he is revealed, whereas humans cannot keep any secrets from him. The cosmological and moral asymmetries are equally overwhelming: God's dominion encompasses the entire universe, while humans are often not even able to keep their own lives in order. Islamic preachers still like to invoke the following edifying image: before the throne of God, the seventh heaven is no larger than a grain of sand; compared to the seventh, the sixth heaven is only as large as a ring in the desert; compared to the sixth, the fifth is also no larger than a ring in the desert and so on, until the first heaven, which the earthlings believe to be all-encompassing when they look up at it – in these humbling sermons for Muslims, the Aristotelian worldview is kept alive poetically and therapeutically. Then one normally asks the individual believer: so how big are you compared to all those things? The correct answer can only be one like the exclamation of Lessing's Saladin: 'I, dust? I, nothing? O God!'[5] Nonetheless, the exegetes do not tire of insisting that God is profoundly close to us and cares for each human being like his own child; and he carries most of the load for the members of his flock, whom he looks after with love and

---

[5] Gotthold Ephraim Lessing, *Nathan the Wise*, Act III, scene 7.

compassion. For the willing, all that is left in this scenario is the role of the servant who, trembling with requited love, places himself at his lord's disposal. This kind of relationship has been referred to in Christian contexts as a 'patriarchy of love', but this expression is more or less applicable to all situations that bear the hallmarks of patriarchy.

The more the believer is taken over by this supremacization of the lord, the more radically he will be inclined to make his own will subject to instructions from above. An intense form of personal supremacism leads to an extremism of the will to obedience that is typical of zealotic movements. The obedience that embraces this intensification extends so far that a servant prepared to go to any lengths will prefer the most rigid laws and the most unpleasant commands, these offering the necessary material to carry out the work of radical subordination. One still finds traces of this servant syndrome everywhere in the world of today: in malign forms, as exemplified most currently by the suicide attack; in intermediate manifestations as observed in worthy zealous systems such as Opus Dei; and in curious variations, for example the rumour among Vaticanists that, under Pope Paul VI, some Vatican City employees even knelt during telephone conversations with their highest superior.[6]

One should note that the disposition referred to does initially make room for non-neurotic intensifications of the idea of service, though the pathological escalations are usually not long in waiting.[7] A product of this type of

---

[6] Karlheinz Deschner, *Opus Diaboli. Fünfzehn unversöhnliche Essays über die Arbeit im Weinberg des Herrn* [Fifteen Inconciliatory Essays on Work in the Lord's Vineyard] (Reinbek: Rowohlt, 2001), p. 173.

[7] As already stated, however, one should not attribute the zeal for God's cause primarily to psychodynamic sources – for example the compulsion to gain the attention of a busy father, a common phenomenon among the over-abundant sons of families with many children. The zealotic disposition can ultimately only be understood with reference to the matrix of personal supremacism, which encourages the intensification of service to its extreme of its own accord.

supremacization that is initially psychologically inconspicuous is an affinity for majesty and splendour, in both moral-political and aesthetic areas. But the irrationalist tendency is also part of the structure: for if God demands sacrifices, why not sacrifice reason too? This is manifest in the willingness to believe that even the deepest darkness contains holy meaning and to obey the instructions from above against all doubts, even – and especially – when the command remains unfathomable, as it was for Abraham when God demanded the sacrifice of his son Isaac. In the realm of the personal supreme power, everything hinges on trust in the integrity of the commander. No one is granted the right to obstinacy. In such a universe, it must sound like an incitement to anarchy when Hannah Arendt, following on from Kant, states: 'No one has the right to obey.'

The history of resorting to the highest also displays an impersonal variant that I will refer to as objective or ontological supremacism. Here, ascent to the pinnacle – as Plato described in his reflections on the stages of rapture, from a single beautiful body to disembodied beauty and goodness 'itself' – brings the believer to a supreme power that does not have the properties of a personal being, but rather those of a principle or an idea. This supremacy, which culminates in a nameless highest being, can only be spoken about in terms of first and final justifications of an object-like, suprapersonal and structural nature. Concisely put: the ascent to the objective highest leads to the god of the philosophers. Even its crudest portraits show that it has little or nothing in common with the Abrahamic versions of God (El, Yahweh, God the Father, Allah).[8] It

---

[8] This observation contrasts starkly with the attempts among Catholic theologians and philosophers to prove – against Pascal – that the god of the philosophers was identical to that of Abraham, Isaac and Jacob. Cf. Robert Spaemann, *Das unsterbliche Gerücht. Die Frage nach Gott und die Täuschung der Moderne* [The Immortal Rumour. The Question of God and the Deception of Modernity] (Stuttgart: Klett-Cotta, 2007), pp. 13f.

is neither creator nor monarch nor judge; it is a source of that which is, and from its unsurpassable bestness radiates a derived best, the cosmos. It does not have the power to command; it has the power of self-revelation through superabundance. Its creative potency realizes itself according to the scheme of a causality through goodness.

The position of human beings in an ontologically and cosmologically supremacized world context therefore can not be interpreted as bondage or willingness to serve. Rather, true being-in-the-world demands an awareness of one's participation in universal systems of order. Now it is a matter of understanding in an advanced sense: an adaptation of the understander to the superior exigencies of being. The ascent takes place on the ladder of general concepts. Therefore God can bear conceptual names such as the *unum*, the *verum*, the *bonum*, the *maximum*, the *simplicissimum* or the *actualissimum*. Even such titles are sufficient to inspire believers – Hegel, Hölderlin and Schelling still swore on the *hen kai pan* [One and All] in their youthful ardour, like revolutionaries on their watchword.

Like the first supremacism, the second also draws believers towards extremes – not in the form of blazing servility, nor a yearning for death in flames as mentioned by Goethe in the subtlest of his Islamically inclined poems, but rather as the willingness to push oneself back to the objective level in order to let things glow of their own accord. This presupposes that the reproduction of these things in the clouded mirror of subjectivity, the interested will and biased sensuality is replaced by an objective, desensualized thinking cleansed of all wilfulness. The ontological supremacism that characterizes Greek – and, even more, Indian – metaphysics releases a passion for depersonalization that can grow into the ambition to merge the human subject with the anonymous origin of the world. While the striving for the personal highest follows the super-you in order to be absorbed fully by its will, the First Philosophy seeks to lose itself in the super-id. Objective supremacism – which, since Heidegger, is often labelled as onto-theology and viewed with suspicion like a subtle form of idolatry – is ultimately concerned with dissolving the subject into a substance.

In order to complete the picture, we should speak of a third supremacism in the old European culture of reason whose point of departure lies in the experience of thought and inner speech – and later also of writing. Here we become acquainted with a second face of philosophy, in so far as the latter can begin with the self-exploration of thinking instead of taking the world as its focus. Since Heraclitus' discovery of the *logos* and the introduction of the concept of *nous* by Anaxagoras, logical or noetic supremacism has been working towards an alternative ascent that leads, in its own way, to the god of the philosophers; but this time not through the north face of substance, but rather along the fine line of spiritual articulations. This line also leads to the One and Ultimate – this time, however, the supreme being is not interpreted from the perspective of substantiality, let alone in terms of majesty and omnipotence. Here it is the all-pervading intelligibility and constructive force of the spiritual principle that lies at the centre. One must be careful to avoid the mistake of equating this non-theologically highest power too readily with the divine attribute of omniscience found in religion. For in terms of its dynamist origin, God's knowledge within the system of personal supremacism possesses, as well as the quality of creation wisdom, the more significant quasi-political function of universal supervision and total bookkeeping of all deeds done and undone by believers and non-believers alike – its decisive application will therefore be on Judgement Day, when God himself opens the files for public viewing. The ascent to the highest, on the other hand, in accordance with noetic supremacism, leads to theoretical perceptions that accompany the divine intellect on its innermost folding into itself and its unfolding into the world. It is not uncommon for mathematics to be brought into play in this sublime endoscopy, as it depicts structures as they are before any sensuality and hence before any subjectively determined ambiguity.

The theory of the highest intellect, like that of being, strives to present itself as strictly supra-personal and beyond the profane human sphere. The extremism that lies in the nature of this matter too manifests itself in a striving for the final formula. It does not let up until the human spirit is granted a connection to the higher intellects, and ultimately even a knowledge of God's procedures in the creation of the world. Even Hegel's seemingly hubristic statement that his logic contained the thoughts God entertained before the creation does not go any further than what is customary in the supremacism of the spirit. Furthermore, Hegel's programme of developing substance as subject perfectly expressed the aim of noetic supremacism. It is part of the long history of Christian receptions of Yahweh's self-assertion: 'I am that I am' (Exodus 3:14). With this, theologians add a divine ego character to the being of the ontologists and allow the human ego to take part in it epicentrically[9] – an operation in which the German Idealists attained mastery. A part of the image of the corresponding extremism is the radicality of the will to a logical penetration of all circumstances that has always characterized pneumatic thinkers. It has often been interpreted as arrogance – though one could equally view it as a higher form of irony. For the partisans of the spirit, most of what issues from the mouths of humans is nothing but inane air movement in any case – just as they almost always consider everyday life a mere rolling around in gravity. To them, the ordinary descendants of Adam are no more than upright worms. What is a human being before it is transformed by the

---

[9] Hence the obsession among theologians from Philo to Augustine with Exodus 3:14, whereas early rabbinical literature shows a complete lack of interest in the *ehyeh asher ehyeh*. Cf. Bloom, *Jesus and Jahweh*, pp. 73f.

spirit? A decorated intestine with God knows what delusions about its own substance. Little wonder that the advocates of such views rarely lack a tendency to logical flights of fancy.

When supremacists of this kind explain themselves, one hears the postulation that where matter was, spirit shall be – or that a planned order of reason must replace the chaos that has grown over time. The third disappearance of humans (following their eradication in the service of the Lord and their dissolution into the anonymous substance) is supposed to be achieved by their spiritual evaporation on the way to the divine omega point. The fact that noetic supremacism has occasionally resembled its substance-ontological partner does not negate its autonomy. In effect it formed a community of tradition with it in which it risked misunderstanding itself substantialistically. This was only brought to a halt by the transcendental shift following Descartes and Kant, that is to say through the depotentization of the theory of intellect to the critique of reason. This approach, as Kurt Flasch has shown in critical interventions, reached one of its most sublime manifestations in the intellect-theoretical speculations of Dietrich von Freiberg and Meister Eckhart, who were inspired by Arab Aristotelianism – in particular Averroes – and are often misinterpreted by the life-philosophically stimulated public in their own country as 'German mystics'.[10] Naturally, the secularization of the intellect inevitably changed the premises of the third supremacism in the wake of the Enlightenment; but the fate of such ideas as the dialectical thinking made current

---

[10] Cf. Kurt Flasch, 'Meister Eckhart – Versuch, ihn aus dem mystischen Strom zu retten' [An Attempt to Save Him from the Mystical Maelstrom] in *Gnosis und Mystik in der Geschichte der Philosophie* [Gnosis and Mysticism in the History of Philosophy], ed. Peter Koslowski (Darmstadt, 1988), pp. 94ff.; also Flasch, *Meister Eckhart. Die Geburt der 'Deutschen Mystik' aus dem Geist der arabischen Philosophie* [The Birth of 'German Mysticism' from the Spirit of Arab Philosophy] (Munich, 2006).

by Hegel has shown that the battle over the interpretation of the cognitively highest still continues in modern times. The tensions between the three leading noetic supremacisms of the twentieth century – the dialectical, the phenomenological and the grammatological – would require an examination of their own.

In the light of what has been said so far, the matrix of logical operations that result in zealotic monotheisms can be shown without much additional effort. I have already hinted that the three supremacisms correspond to three extremisms that should be understood as three ways of overcoming resistance to a union with the One and Only. The methods, praised as 'realizations', of eliminating the human will in service, substance and spiritualization share a positivization of death, in so far as death offers the most direct route to the Lord, to being and to the spirit. The question of whether an affirmation of death should be assigned symbolic or literal meaning may remain unanswered. None of the resolute have ever contradicted the statement that some form of self-elimination is a prerequisite for reaching higher regions. Albert Camus's thesis that suicide is the central philosophical problem shows that its originator was one of the dying breed of metaphysically talented authors in the twentieth century, and the sneering of some philosophically unmusical thinkers only served to underline this.

The extremisms, for their part, are especially consistent applications of high cultural grammar, which was based on the rigid combination of a monovalent ontology and a bivalent logic. Monovalence of speech about that which is means: the things of which it is said that they are actually are, and are not not; nor are they anything other than what they are. Hence they share in being, both in the fact *that* and the fact of *what* and *how*. Hence they can best be expressed in tautologies. In this area one cannot aspire to originality, and if one is asked what being is, one should – referring to Heidegger – simply answer that it is itself. In the realm of monovalence a rose is a rose, and it lies in its nature that it flowers without any reason or consideration for its observer. The only other things that meet such strict standards of identity are the choirs of angels when they exalt the Highest in a monovalent language. This language forms a medium that neither requires nor permits contradictions, nor does it show any weak spots that could allow an infiltration by error, false statements or unstable structures. Thus the angels can speak eternal truth about eternal being. Unlike human ontologists, they never risk missing the point when they praise God.

Terrestrial speakers dream in vain of such achievements, as our languages are destined to be bivalent in their constitution. It is not inconceivable that, before the expulsion from Eden, Adam's language also consisted purely of adequate names and well-formed affirmations, so that everything he uttered in paradise became a natural hymn to that which is. The expulsion introduced a second value, however; indeed, logicians view the myth of the banishment of Adam and Eve from the garden of identity as no less than a poetic attempt to narrate the growth of human reflection as a tragedy. This is not implausible, for whoever eats their daily bread in the sweat of their brow will separate the true from the false even as they frown – a burden that can be compared to the curse of farming. Let us note, then, that the first negation came not from the human spirit, but rather from God's command *not* to eat from the tree.

The introduction of this second value made the human capacity for true statements unstable, as these – being a reflection in the other of that which is – were now accompanied by the fatal possibility of being false. The fact that the capacity for untruth clings to the act of statement is one of freedom's dowries – if freedom means being exposed, in a postlapsarian state, to the inclination to speak falsely, whether due to an honest mistake, for strategic reasons or simply out of an enjoyment of untruth for its own sake. Even if one takes pains to present things in – as far as we can establish it – the way their own state dictates, one should fundamentally expect some gap through which falsehood can enter. Metaphorically expressed, the true sentence does not grow on the branch of real conditions – it is no growth at all, no continuation of what naturally is in what naturally is. Rather, sentences are always, in a way that is specific to humans, artificial, daring and unnatural – in fact, they are always potentially perverse. According to the majority tradition of the classical logicians, they constitute a reflection of nature in a more or less murky medium, that is to say mirrorings that lack any substantial weight of their own, and are thus in constant danger of multiplying the host of phantoms. How else could one interpret the fact that for every true statement, there are an infinite number of possible false ones? What does a sentence mean in the cosmos anyway? It seems like a necessary, but fundamentally hazardous, supplement that, with an artificial effort and an inevitable delay, joins the collection of things that truly are. A sentence is always so remote from that which is that its formulation inevitably risks missing the mark. One can turn it on its head and back again, one can stretch, twist and squash it, and nothing seems simpler than making it express the opposite of its actual intention. In the best case, the double negation leads back to the original sentence, though even this may itself also have been false. Under such circumstances, how is it that one occasionally has the impression certain statements are nonetheless true and correct? Probably only because particular speakers manage to evade the danger and temptation to present falsehoods, clinging instead to those aspects on the side of being that seem to be in a state of simple identity with themselves, as if there were no mistaken, deceitful or self-contradictory people – or, in the jargon of philosophers: as if the identical could be represented undistorted in the non-identical, or as if being could be transformed into corresponding signs without any loss of substance.

Now we can clarify what the zealotic monotheisms and their universalist missions mean from a logical perspective. They rest on the intention of eliminating the risk of failure introduced by the second value at all costs – even if that implies removing the errant along with the error. In fact the errant himself, viewed in terms of the ideal of monovalent being and its reflection in the true sentence, is merely a form of real nothingness whose liquidation is no great loss – just as the *massif* of being continues to exist unharmed, as it was and will be, whenever an incorrect statement about one of its details is annulled.

This disposition is, as we have seen, given through the combination of classical ontology and classical logic. If the second value is only a reflexive one, a value that enables a surplus of potentially untenable statements and superfluous negations beyond the number of real facts counted out by being or by God himself (but also serves to verify these, as Plato's dialogues show), it should suffice to eliminate the parasitic sentences, the lies, the errors, the ideological and the fictitious, and if need be also the accompanying speakers, in order to bring human speech back to the core content of legitimate statements – legitimate, as we have seen, because they are supported by being and spawned by the spirit in the spirit. Essentially, all supremacist zealots have only one concern: the mission of expelling the insolent traders from the temple of monovalence. Does Dante Alighieri not tell us that everything superfluous displeases God and nature?[11] The necessity of such an intervention becomes evident as soon as, owing to various requirements of the evolution of ideas (warning: axial age!), a strictly monovalent ontology is systematically bound together with a strictly bivalent logic.

This configuration permits the first appearance of the phenomenon of strictness. When strictness coincides with lack of complexity, zealotry is in its element. Thinking becomes strict as soon as it insists that only one of two

---

[11] Dante, *Monarchia*, I, 14.

options can be right for us. Then it guards its cause jealously to make sure that the side of being is taken, not of nothingness; of the essential, not of the inessential; of the Lord, not of the lordless and lawless. The logical origin of zealotry lies in bringing everything down to the number one, which tolerates no one and nothing beside itself. This number one is the mother of intolerance. It demands the radical *either* in which the *or* is ruled out. Whoever says 'two' is saying one too many. *Secundum non datur.*

These reflections take us into the deep structure of the iconoclastic syndrome. If the rigid monotheisms frown upon the use of images, this is not simply because they embody the danger of idolatry. More importantly, the unacceptable nature of images stems from the observation that they never serve purely to reproduce that which is represented, but always assert their own significance in addition. The autonomous value of the second aspect as such becomes visible in them – and the iconoclasts will go to any lengths to destroy this. They empathize with a God who has regretted his creation ever since his creatures began to have minds of their own. They come to his aid by exterminating whatever distracts the creatures from an exclusive bond to the One. As humans 'misuse' their freedom to craft images, the iconoclasts wish to put an end to this misuse by restricting the creatures' freedom by force. This is supposedly done to show humans the way back to the true God. In reality, however, iconoclasm seeks to attack the autonomy of the world, in so far as 'world' represents the epitome of the emancipated second aspect. In iconoclasm, which is actually a cosmoclasm, one finds the articulation of a resentment of any human freedom that is not prepared to accept immediate self-denial and obedience.

The zealotic monotheisms (like the zealotic Enlightenment and zealotic scientism in later times) draw their momentum from the fantastic notion that they could succeed, in the face of all the delusions and confusions of our controversially lingualized and multiply pictorialized reality, in 'reinstating' a monovalent primal language. They want to make audible the monologue of things as they are, and reproduce the unconcealed facts, the first structures, the purest instructions of being, without having to address the intermediate world of languages, images and projections with its independent logic. The followers of the revelational religions even seek to make the monologue of God himself reverberate in the human ear, the listener being a mere recipient who does not involve his own ego – and hence does not acquire any share in the author's rights.

Now one can also understand why there need to be several varieties of zealotry. Depending on the type of supremacization they tend towards, their agents choose typical procedures for returning from ambiguity to certainty, from the fallibility of idle talk to the infallibility of the original text. At any rate, the aim of this motto of 'back to a time before reflection!' is to block out human language as it was spoken after the Fall. Its replacement is a code still untarnished by the negations, contradictions and capacity for error inherent in bivalent speech. Hence the interest of logical, moral and religious extremists in a language beyond human speech. In striving for the extra-human and superhuman, the religious zealots join hands with the mathematical rigorists, and the advocates of self-dissolution within being also follow along.

The oldest and most enduring examples of how to return from the post-Adamite position to the humanly impossible monovalent language can be found in early monotheistic prophethood. This is no surprise, as the prophets claimed to express nothing more than God's view of the world, not their own personal opinions. The prophetic word begins interventionistically and ends absolutistically: it contradicts what specific people do or say in specific situations – yet it cannot be contradicted by anything, as it claims to come from a sphere devoid of reflection or second opinions. The word borrowed from the Highest, then conveyed by the speaker to the unjust prince or the misguided people, is no mere village gossip. It brings every debate to an end by saying what is and what should be. It appears to be critique – some modern theologians like to exalt prophecy as the source of social critique – but, as monovalence does not allow the critical word, any egalitarian debate or expression of opinion, it becomes the last word on the matter – not dramaturgically, before an audience, but rather eschatologically, before the Highest.

Alphabetization takes care of the rest. The founding of great religions takes place, as has often been observed, on the boundary between medial galaxies. The classical prophets, from Moses to Mohammed, are located on the thresholds between regimes of cultural memory. Medially musical, they play upon two instruments while allowing themselves to be played upon from both sides. They look back into the universe of orality and make its legends and trances sound ('speaking means playing with the other's body', according to Alfred Tomatis); at the same time, they look ahead to scriptural culture and bring forth its hidden relationships between literality and truth. They testify to the pressure of coherence that increases through scripturality, and to everything else that accompanies the 'advances in spirituality' caused by alphabetization. The central concern, however, is that the great mediators themselves want to be viewed as living texts. What is a prophet if not a registered letter to humanity? He embodies a piece of writing whose receipt is often refused and which, once accepted, can usually not be read correctly by its first recipients. Not reading correctly: that means treating the undeniable text as if it were a debatable one, a text on which salvation depends like an everyday document. If a prophet is without honour in his own country, it is because nobody can believe that 'one of us' can change over to the realm of monovalence overnight.

Describing Judaism, Christianity and Islam as prophetic religions means observing that they constitute three stages of God's inlibration – and if the book seemed for an aeon to have been assigned a metaphysical surplus value, this was not least because it could be seen as a vehicle for the absolute. One can consider the monotheisms pure religions of faith if faith refers to the internal operations through which believers act in relation to the inlibrated God. They are usually acts of inner collection to prepare one for the encounter with the overwhelming – and why not also with the disarmingly simple? Through faith, the infinite regress of doubt and a drifting in unbelief is stopped. It helps to secure a foundation from which all other thoughts and actions can 'emanate'.[12]

The paths of the believers diverge when it becomes time to decide whether the word of God is not only monovalent, but also monolingual, as Islam states in its doctrine of divine Qur'anic Arabic (and as, slightly further in the background, the Cabbalists also claim in their accounts of God experimenting with Hebrew letters during the creation), or whether monovalence and multilinguality can coexist, as Christians believe. In fact, the tale of Pentecost provides the latter with the paradigm of a multilingual and monovalent spiritual outpouring – which could justify an initial suspicion of intellectual and communicative superiority. They diverge even further faced with the question of how close God and humans, or the book and humans, are allowed to get to each other: while Jews and Muslims remove God to the realm of the incomparable and carefully allow humans to approach the book, Christianity created a transitive *ménage à trois*. Here the inlibration of God is replaced by his incarnation. Hence further transitions are pre-programmed, and their unfolding is only a matter of time and conjuncture.[13]

---

[12] Translator's note: there is an ambiguity in the original – encouraged by the quotation marks – through the use of the word *ausgehen*, which can mean both 'to emanate' and 'to (pre)suppose'.

[13] In this matrix there are six possible messages: rejoice, for God has become man; God has become the book; man has become God; man has become the book; the book has become God; the book has become man. The use of this field for alternative gospels is to be expected, especially if one takes into account that 'book' can be replaced with 'machine'.

In terms of its history and its subject, prophetism belongs to the category of personal supremacism. It calls upon its participants to submit completely to the word of the Lord; in the best case, this submission takes place in the mode of comprehending conformation. In Islam, God has the sole rights to the holy text, being its author (Mohammed acts as a radiant model of the pure medium); in Christianity they are transferred to Christ as the co-author ('the eternal word of the father'); while Jewish scriptural scholars sometimes act as if the prophets had given notable interviews to which the rights, if they cannot be completely in the hands of the interviewer, should at least be divided equally among the partners. All variations show a clear hierarchical difference between the sender and the recipient. The pronouncements from above are received as revelations and preserved in sacredly guarded copies. They are read in a cultic context, and exegetes carry out their interpretations on their knees in constant fear of blasphemy. It was only with the reformers of the sixteenth century that laypersons were permitted to read the scriptures; the Enlightenment thinkers of the seventeenth and eighteenth centuries went further, making it possible to profane them with impunity by securing the freedom to engage in non-cultic, even critical, interpretation.

Objective or ontological supremacism, on the other hand, cannot possess any holy scriptures for internal reasons. It points quietly to the library of classics, whose statements remain within the sphere of the debatable, even when dealing with first and last things. If one were to give individual authors, for example Plato, such epithets as 'the divine', this would display a mixture of effusiveness and calculation. When it comes to philosophers, one tends to be closer friends with the truth than with the author who formulated it. Pure being is certainly nothing that can be blasphemed – which is why someone who desires to mock it need not fear any reprisals: to those in the know, it is obvious that ignorance is its own punishment.

A double penalty would be beneath philosophy (to say nothing of the infamy of asymmetrical punishment in the zealotic religions, which like to repay finite offences with infinite penitential suffering). The ascent to monovalence occurs here with the calmness that is native to positivism as a whole. Its mantra: 'it is what it is'[14] – for, may Erich Fried forgive us, it is not love that says this, but rather a wisdom undistorted by a desire for anything different. It views things as it finds them, and lets them be what they are for the meantime – the question of how they are altered will arise soon enough. Ontological positivism moves effortlessly from each corner of what is into silence. The highest, to which this silence refers, is the whole, as it is for itself when there are no subjective, negative or reflexive impulses to distort it. The substance is always what it is – the good, which presents itself in sublime neutrality, or the perfect, which we encounter in the guise of the ordinary. Not forgetting that even a grain of sand is what it is, because, on its own level and in its own way, it participates in the convergence of being and being good.

Above all else, however, substance is discreet. It does not demand the christening of children and advises against book burnings. It would send pilgrims home, as Santiago, Lourdes or Mecca cannot be any closer to it than any other point in space. There is, as mentioned above, no known bible of objective supremacism. If there were such a thing, it would be substance itself in written form; but how can one conceive of writing, this supplement to a supplement to a supplement, in such an essential role – this near-nothing of ink, which fixes a near-nothing of sound, which is turn articulates a near-nothing made from aspects of consciousness through modulations of the air? The answers

---

[14] From Erich Fried's poem 'Was es ist': 'Es ist Unsinn / sagt die Vernunft / Es ist, was es ist / sagt die Liebe' [It is nonsense / says reason / It is what it is / says love']: Erich Fried, *'Es ist was es ist.' Liebesgedichte, Angstgedichte, Zorngedichte* [Love Poems, Fear Poems, Anger Poems] (Berlin: Wagenbach, 1996).

to these questions are to be found primarily among the Hegelians, who, for their project of developing substance as subject, can use anything that helps to dissolve the block of being into subtler relationships.

In the thinking of being, it is this last thought that is the most dangerous. The substance of the philosophers does not become a curse for those who dissect or ignore it; it only sucks in those who have understood enough about it to seek absolute immersion in it. Ontological extremism becomes attractive for the spirited, the nervous, whose constitution reduces their chances of finding peace in being. It is the most pathos-laden and contemplative searchers who espouse an apathetic, unreflexive substance most ardently. They have the loftiest ideas about the block of silence, which they want to resemble yet are so unlike. In their reflexivity and agitation, they take themselves for the blemish that taints being. Finally, they seek to combat the disturbance of the substance's peace within them by eliminating the subject that is in the way – namely themselves. These martyrs of ontology want to pull off the trick of dissolving the non-idiocy of the human condition in the idiocy of pure being. If philosophy has its own form of piety, it is found in such sacrifices. Heidegger's well-known statement against the god of the philosophers – namely that, being the fetish of the self-spawning substance, it is a god to whom one cannot pray – omits the possibility of dissolving oneself in this very god.[15] It is furthermore, with all due respect, an objection of limited wisdom, for the feeling of belonging to a great whole and the anticipation of returning to it are the natural prayer of contemplative intelligence.

It is telling that India has not only provided a home for the most radical holy fools, but also been a fertile environment for the most extreme ontologies since time immemorial. The ones found in Greece were only ever the

---

[15] Cf. Martin Heidegger, *Identity and Difference*, trans. Joan Stambaugh (Chicago: University of Chicago Press, 2002).

shallower varieties, as the Greeks – like Mediterraneans in general, if such blanket statements are permitted – have little talent for extremism. Only Empedocles, the yogi among the Hellenes, strove for an enlightened suicide – not without making sure, in an act of effect-aesthetic alertness, that his sandal, left behind in the crater of Mount Etna, would provide evidence of the all-signifying leap into being. The European sceptics did not fail to note that piece of footwear left behind at the moment of the holy marriage of subject and substance – and this doubt was still alive centuries later, when Brecht glossed the account of the sandal trick with suspicion; even later, Bazon Brock suggested re-enacting it by means of a disclosive performance. What is being if it leaves such a blatant remainder? It would take aeons to find an adequate answer – it can be calculated by adding the remainder to the whole. This operation deprives being of its supposed simplicity – it now transpires as the non-one, cleft by nothingness, a more-than-whole and simultaneously less-than-whole. From this moment on, its primitive monovalence is a thing of the past. Such concepts were to be reserved for late periods, however – times in which people would say of God that he was not even one with himself, and had thus given up his transcendental reserve and opted for finitude and the capacity for suffering. It was only with the Christologists of the twentieth century that such thoughts could be uttered – by scholars who made no secret of their conviction that God, being entirely of the world beyond, could only profit from becoming human. From the fifth century BC, however, the philosophers in the Hellenic hemisphere pursued careers as educators, orators and moral trainers in the name of the well-ordered essential cosmos. Despite Plato's melancholy and Aristotle's sourness, none were ever allowed to question their status as worldlings.

The Indian ontologies, by contrast, branched out early on into highly divergent schools, each of which produced its own self-effacement artists. It became apparent that

Greek thinking too was not without extremist potential when non-Greeks intervened – such as the African Plotinus and his followers. These were followed by the post-Greek zealots, especially Christian theologians and Arab metaphysicians, whose reception of the supremacism of being and spirit served its fusion with the religiously established supremacism of service to a personal god. This constellation has been referred to as the encounter of Athens and Jerusalem or the gradual Hellenization of Christianity – often without taking into account that, for centuries, the encounter of Athens and Mecca, or, more generally speaking, an urbanization of Islam through Greek theory, had been no less of an issue. Combining different procedures of effacement was the order of the day for the cultivated zealots of the time – they searched for ways to co-ordinate self-dissolution in being or spirit with self-consumption in service to the Lord. It should be noted that these dialogues between cities are among the most influential in earlier intellectual history. The summit meetings of the self-effacers spawned hybrid extremists who combined several supreme authorities. They led to waves of new recruits – first for the monastic orders of Egypt, Syria and Old Europe, then for the crusaders who renounced their selves for Jerusalem, and finally for the early modern partisans of the *imitatio Christi*, who have been described as mystics. Their contemporary descendants have been satirized by Bazon Brock as 'God-seeker gangs' in his critique of art religion. They embody the organized form of an unwillingness to count to three.

6

The pharmaka

If we glance back from this point in our reflections to the alarm signal provided at the start by Derrida's sudden thesis ('The war over the "appropriation of Jerusalem" is today's world war. It is taking place everywhere . . .'[1]), it becomes apparent that the warning sign and the danger spot do not go together. The phrase 'world war' evokes misleading associations – as if three monotheistic army columns were marching towards Jerusalem, each determined to conquer the city for one flag, one book and one credo. But the fact that Christians are no longer interested in possessing Jerusalem already invalidates this notion – even Catholics now side with Hegel in his statement that an empty grave holds nothing in store for Christians except inevitable disappointment. The religious power with the most followers does not come into the equation, then, in the supposed battle over Jerusalem (the presence in the holy city of the monotheisms of a few Christian Zionists who want to be in the front row when Christ returns is of purely anecdotal value), and it is questionable whether a world war without Christians is worthy of such a bombastic title. Profanely speaking, the reality is that Israelis and Palestinians are fighting over the capital city of a real and a virtual state. Religiously speaking, Jews and

---
[1] Cf. above, p. 2.

Muslims are fighting over control of various holy sites: roughly 5½ million people on one side and by now a similar number on the other, together amounting to barely more than half the population of Tokyo or Mexico City. One could only speak of a 'world war' with a large dose of metaphorical freedom – or if one wished to propose that the Israeli–Palestinian conflict is a façade concealing an all-consuming intra-Arab and intra-Islamic civil war that, largely unnoticed by the rest of the world, has so far claimed some 10 million lives and may possibly cost several times as many before it is over, if the dark predictions of Middle East military experts and demographers prove accurate. But that is a matter for a different discussion.

One must therefore assume that Derrida either went astray or was referring to something else. It is probably the second notion that takes us along the right path. In referring to the numerous militant appropriations of Jerusalem, the founder of deconstruction, which produces a critique of the manic element of violence in 'texts', was thinking less of the physical occupation of that territory than an access to the exemplary transmitting station for universalist missions. 'Appropriating Jerusalem': under late monotheistic conditions, that can only mean seeking to take hold of certain symbolic potentials that authorize their bearers to embark on campaigns of the global kind described above. If one chooses the city of the Wailing Wall, the Church of the Holy Sepulchre and the Dome of the Rock as the historical capital of messianic complexes, one can immediately see why there is more than one party that wants to seize, under the code word 'Jerusalem', the privilege of splitting mankind into those who are For Us and those who are Against Us. The world was, and still is, full of minorities that claim to constitute humanity and are anticipating the kingdom. It is teeming with chosen peoples, including more than a few who contest the declared chosen people's prerogative. There is also no shortage of messianisms that see the Lord coming

THE PHARMAKA

from this direction or that. The fact that Derrida thought first of the liberal messianism of certain American ideologues, who had concluded from the recent implosion of the Soviet Union that the 'Western way of life' had triumphed, lends his critical-explosive reverie concrete geopolitical content. What he considered dangerous and repulsive was the confiscation of messianic rhetoric by representatives of a saturated imperialism, as if politicians and their speechwriters were now claiming the right to stammer about the Kingdom come like drunken Adventists. Next to the positive philosophers and embedded journalists, who marched both verbally and physically into the countries of the disbanded Second World with the liberal troop, Derrida was naturally also thinking of the Middle Eastern scene, where anti-Israeli and anti-Jewish confessions led by old and new Arab zealots have become rampant – in their case, the 'appropriation of Jerusalem' would not occur without a corresponding dispossession. One should not rule out the possibility that Derrida was also referring to the Christian Right in the USA, in which the apocalyptic sects and their obligatory 'battle for Jerusalem' rants are increasingly setting the tone.[2]

In the current competition of manic propulsive systems, it is only useful to cite the name 'Jerusalem' to the extent that it refers to a certain amount of that supremacist potential which transforms the world into the scene of religious and ethical campaigns. It is not sufficient in this field to name only one symbolic address, as a considerable number of enthusiastic projects and revivals to force an overarching meaning are currently underway. On the global scale, there are probably several hundred, maybe even several thousand of them (a significant proportion

---

[2] Cf. Victor and Victoria Trimondi, *Krieg der Religionen. Politik, Glaube und Terror im Zeichen der Apokalypse* [The War of Religions. Politics, Faith and Terror Under the Sign of the Apocalypse] (Munich: Fink [Wilhelm], 2006).

of these are Christian-evangelical, neo-Gnostic, para-Hinduist, apocalyptic-Islamist, neo-Communist and syncretistic sects, which all share the same high, manic drive), though only a few attain the status of world-famous spiritual brands. Together with Rome, Mecca, Wittenberg and names of a similar quality, Jerusalem represents the quintessence of personal supremacism. It is from such centres that the ecstasies of the will to serve are sent out into the world. From a positive point of view, some of these toponyms indicate a widening of empathetic circles: they testify to the increasing ability of religiously and idealistically motivated people to take an interest in the fates of strangers as if they were relatives.

In the following I intend to show why the battle over the 'appropriation of Jerusalem' will not take the form of an inter-monotheistic war. Certainly we are witnesses of, and to a degree also combatants in, a conflict on a 'spiritual front', yet the gravity and inevitability of the current collisions do not result from what has been referred to in the debates of recent years as the 'clash of monotheisms'. The battle is concerned far more with how to ensure control of the extremist potentials within each of the zealotically disposed religions – and the raging ideologies that came after the universalist religions. I say control, not elimination, as such tensions cannot be made to disappear, only diverted into less harmful expressions. In so far as the aforementioned extremisms regularly arise from the applications of personal supremacism to the lives and environments of the zealots, diverting in practice means: working to dampen the extremism of service at the centre of those movements that desire to plunge into the extreme. This demands a decoupling of affect and religious code; the risk of becoming a zealot oneself in the fight against zealotry is an occupational hazard here. Whoever participates with sufficient expertise in the de-supremacization of the supremacisms must get close to their burning centres.

The first step in this process is to show that the concept of the Highest is only useful as an upper limit – and therefore cannot belong to anyone or be appropriated by any 'representative' or 'successor', any custodian of faith, in an exclusive manner. One would think this an easy hurdle to clear, as it hardly seems conceivable that anyone could believe themselves in a position to put their own stamp on the supreme power. And one must even maintain this objection when the greatest good is 'evident' as the revealed word of God. Such things, it would seem, are part of the ABC of any theology and should be assertable everywhere without any great effort. A brief glance around, however, shows how little the mindset of the actors on the current zealotic stages confirms these assumptions.

The reflections on the intertwinement of logic and ontology in the monotheisms developed above show that the task to which I have referred as de-supremacization does not lie in the jurisdiction of psychologists. Rather, it must begin with a logical clarification – at least in the first round. This is the only way to obtain the pharmaka that will help combat supremacist fury. The long-term goal is admittedly more challenging: it must lie in dissolving the time-honoured matrix in which monovalently conceived being is necessarily and compulsively joined with the positive value of the bivalently conceivable statement. This system, as we have seen, was responsible for the numerous historically documented attempts to impose monovalent information from without and above by eliminating the negative value. One need hardly point out that the terror of our own times still functions according to this scheme.

The familiar methods developed in advanced civilizations for reaching authoritative, monovalent theses – whether through an oracle, mathematics or the theory of forms, through prophecy, illumination, informative trance or finally through such doctrines as the incarnation of the word or the inlibration of God – were all characterized by a striving to break out of the sphere of fallible knowledge, to anchor human existence eccentrically in the absolute. Its aim was always an *inconcussum* that would be reached not through the introspective self-confirmation of the subject, but rather by ecstatically overwhelming it. A foundation is considered unshakeable once it makes the breakthrough to an absolute anchor point. In order to force access to this, absolutists use a sleight of hand that, though always the same in formal terms, allows material executions in many directions: they choose the exaggeration of passivity as the ideal path of being. The word 'being' here refers to the totality of connections that encompasses, reaches through and validates us mortals. If one is to find some point of orientation from without, passive ecstasy is indispensable. How else should one attain such a state than through the postulation that, when playing with God or being, there are throws where humans catch something they have not thrown themselves – not even as ricochets of their own throws?[3] At the decisive moment, the person who catches the ball is supposed to be a pure recipient and nothing but a recipient. If he goes about it correctly, he is no longer himself in the instant of catching, but rather the medium of a transcendental sender. What he receives is then supposed to determine everything else – even the profane states following the ecstasy, in which it is once more his turn to serve the ball.

One can state, in the most cordial possible tone, that every one of the aforementioned figures used to force such a pure reception has become problematic. This becomes

---

[3] Translator's note: this is a reference to a poem written by Rainer Maria Rilke in 1922. It begins 'Solange du Selbstgeworfenes fängst, ist alles Schicklichkeit und lässlicher gewinn', and the published translation of the full poem reads as follows – 'As long as you catch self-thrown things / it's all dexterity and venial gain – ; / only when you've suddenly caught that ball / which she, one of the eternal players, / has tossed toward you, your center, with / a throw precisely judged, one of those arches / that exist in God's great bridge-system: / only then is catching a proficiency, – / not yours, a world's': Rainer Maria Rilke, *Uncollected Poems*, trans. Edward Snow (San Francisco: North Point Press, 1996).

clearest whenever there is an attempt to reinstate them. Either one tries to find substitute forms of plausibility, usually taken from anthropology, sociology or psychoanalysis, or one supports one's defence using means that go subversively beyond the horizon of what is actually being defended. But even if conservative thinking has always chosen refinement in order to preserve the simple, that simplicity is damaged by its conservation. That applies equally to the need to cling to the myth of passivity. If one is to recognize the role of the radical monotheisms in moral and cognitive evolution, it is only fair to meet them on the field of their own strengths – their greatest, however, the apparent predication on the foundations of religious and ontological authority, consists (as noted above) in precarious methods of forcibly obtaining transcendent information. If one follows these procedures all the way back to their tangible origins, the strengths turn into weakness. The authorities regularly transpire as borrowers who are unconcerned with paying their debts as long as they have the power to intimidate the trusting lenders. However good one's intentions may be, the results of an examination are unequivocal. After a comprehensive acknowledgement of all the evidence, after listening patiently to the witnesses and advocates, the conclusion is inescapable: the matrix of traditional religious and philosophical metaphysical systems has been exhausted. On the one hand, 'exhausted' means fully developed and realized, while on the other it means entirely used up and seen through in its fundamentally limited and erroneous nature.

In this situation, the path of polyvalent thinking is the only viable one. It is hardly necessary to explain the meaning of polyvalence to interested parties as if it were a complete novelty; any non-pedantic form of intelligence practises it implicitly from childhood, with reference to both things and ideas. While traditional logic stands or falls with the dictum *tertium non datur* (there is no third option between yes and no), everyday thinking has always found ways to reach precisely such a *tertium datur*.[4] The universal procedure in this field is the de-radicalization of alternatives: if one confronts someone with an *either/or* they consider unwelcome, one will observe how they remodel it into a *both-and* sooner or later. If one removes all colours from the world – an assumption that, as Oliver Sacks has shown, does apply for some people on the 'island of the colour-blind'[5] – the result will be a visually trivalent universe in which a halfway world of graded shades of grey mediates between the extremes of white and black. This may seem trivial, and yet it is informative in the present context. Grey here means a release from the obligation to choose between black and white. It embodies the reality of thirdness. In a world characterized by shades of grey, furthermore, one can predict the appearance of extremists who, weary of intermediate values, fight for a pure black or white world. If a party of radicals comes to power, the grey option will be declared counter-revolutionary propaganda. Generations may pass before a change in the wind once more permits an open espousal of the grey world's merits.

The terrain of the zealotic monotheisms also contains occasions for a transition to polyvalent thinking. Islam in particular, normally known for its pathos of strict monovalence, achieved an exemplary breakthrough in the creation of a third value. This took place when it was decreed that people of the book no longer had to choose between

---

[4] Cf. Klaus Heinrich, *Tertium datur: eine religionsphilosophische Einführung in die Logik* [A Religion-Philosophical Introduction to Logic] (Basle: Stroemfeld, 1981). In addition to the non-technical arguments for polyvalence hinted at here, one should also point out the technical analysis of polyvalent logical structures in the work of Lukasiewisc and the Polish school, as well as in recent computer science. Gotthard Günther has taken a path of his own to establish a non-Aristotelian logic, though so far his work has been read more by systems theorists than philosophers.
[5] Oliver Sacks, *The Island of the Colour-blind* (London: Picador, 1997).

the Qur'an and death. The creation of *dhimmi* status, which effectively constitutes subjugation without conversion, established a third option between a yes or no to the Muslim cult. This has occasionally been misunderstood as a form of tolerance – a fairly un-Islamic concept, as well as a fairly un-Catholic one – whereas it should sooner be understood as a primitive manifestation of polyvalent thinking. For the subjugated it was tantamount to survival, while for the subjugators it meant the discovery of a way to circumvent the duty of mass murder. If the Islamic leaders had applied the alternative specifically prescribed by their laws – conversion or liquidation – to the many millions of Christians and the Jewish minorities that became subjects of Arab rulers in the seventh and eighth centuries (when the Byzantine Empire, as noted above, lost half of its population to expanding Islam), this would have led to the greatest bloodbath in the history of mankind. The realization that God, the merciful one, could not have wanted this, and that the elimination of useful subjects would also have weakened Arab power interests, would not have been especially problematic for the Islamic scholars of the time. So they made use of the classic tool by which intellectuals solve an unwelcome dilemma: they de-radicalized the alternative by inventing a middle option. Accordingly they introduced a poll tax (*jizya*, which would have been roughly the same as the tithe) for Jews, Christians and followers of Zoroaster; hence these groups were set apart from Muslims, who had a duty to give alms (*zakat*), but made equal to them in other respects – like scholars, treasuries are quick to learn the ways of polyvalence.

One can observe something formally comparable centuries later in medieval Europe, when Christian theologians had to grapple with the task of toning down the terror factor in the alternative of salvation or eternal damnation that had been in force since Augustine. The theme was dictated by a change in the 'zeitgeist' – if it is permissible to transfer a concept from the early nineteenth century to circumstances in the twelfth and thirteenth. From that era on, it became clear that the inhabitants of the reforming European towns were no longer prepared to accept the psycho-politics of holy terror that had gone unchallenged until then. The change of consciousness was a harbinger of the Reformation, in the broader sense of the word – if one takes it to mean the restructuring of the Christian church according to the demands of an urban clientele that had gained literacy and self-confidence, and was no longer a priori subservient or susceptible to intimidation. Such people are able to plan, calculate and give orders; they have a sense of proportion and possess a clear idea of business on a reciprocal basis. They do not trade with half the world and lead moderate, active lives full of sacrifices in the proud restrictions of guild structures to have some gloomy cathedral preachers threaten them with the horrors of everlasting damnation.

Faced with the discrepancy between supply and demand, the theologians of the High Middle Ages realized how unbearably crude their eschatological teachings were. Finally they resorted to the method that becomes necessary in such situations: they de-radicalized the alternative and created a third value by expanding the realm beyond this life to include a purifying hell, better known as purgatory. By inventing this third place in the twelfth and thirteenth centuries, the designers of the Christian doctrine of last things managed to remodel the system of religious intimidation in such a way that there would still be sufficient terror to maintain control of the spiritual lives of believers, yet without completely snubbing their increased expectations of moderation, coherence and respect for their achievements. Part of the dangerous secret of Augustinism that lay hidden in the doctrine of grace from 397 could now be aired: now one could, in most cases, replace eternal hell with the purifying hell, a place open to all sinners – except for the irretrievable candidates for Lucifer's kingdom. Only those who had been transfigured during their lifetimes – if anyone –

would be exempted from this post-mortal follow-up treatment in the new regime; in their cases, even heaven itself could not turn down the call of *paradiso subito*. The decisive fact was that the creation of purgatory marked the establishment of a third option between the inferno and paradise that assumed characteristics of both places: the grisly décor and gruesome punishments of hell, but also the confidence and the certainty of a favourable conclusion found in heaven. At the same time, the notion of purgatory lent weight to the highly influential idea that, after death, souls entered a transitional period between the first and second lives – assuming they belonged to the main group of middling sinners with a realistic chance in the hereafter. This marked the first religious appearance of the motif of a 'second life'. It was only a matter of time before someone would ask: why should there not be a similar intermediate period before death as well? One only need to have believed in purgatory long enough to believe in history one day – that second goddess in the post-Christian world of ideas who conquered the European stage towards the end of the eighteenth century (the first goddess had borne the promising name of Fortuna and, since the Renaissance, has been present whenever humans raise their standards for a life before death). To live in 'history' can only occur to people who are convinced they are existing in a third time: a necessarily uncomfortable phase of transition between hereditary misery and a promised era of happiness and fulfilment.

The practice of de-supremacization can be traced back to the early phases of the expanding monotheisms, when extremism was still viewed as arrogance and any attempts to reach directly for the highest seemed to be the devil's work. Interest in controlling religious excesses was an automatic result of the force applied in the institutionalization of the exclusive monotheisms. Such religions discovered early on that it was necessary to suppress the same prophetic fire from which they had come, but without extinguishing it. The secret of their survival lay in their ability to curb their inherent immoderation by methods that were in their own repertoire. They had to become Classical in order to ritually absorb the Romanticism from which they had sprung – assuming one can typologically assign their initial apocalyptic upheavals, without which both Christianity and Islam would be inconceivable, to the Romantic end of the spectrum. From this perspective, those religions that subjected themselves to thorough dogmatic reflection provide the best antidotes to their own endogenous excesses – as well as their secularized versions and political parodies. This is the source of the hope that Islam will one day deal with the political metastases so rampant today in the same way earlier Christianity dealt with its Anabaptist and evangelical excesses, the Jacobin cult of the highest being, and finally also with the atheist church of Communism. What is here referred to as monotheistic Classicism has always included – alongside the ubiquitous reminders of the humbling duties of believers – a series of spiritual exercises that contributed implicitly to overcoming the dangerous rigidity of the founding matrix. Among the most notable preparatory disciplines in formal plurivalent thinking are the principles of hierarchical steps and negative theology, then hermeneutics as the art of reading from a variety of perspectives, and last but not least the development of monotheistic humour.

Thinking in steps, which had already combined the doctrine of being with spirit-metaphysical supremacism in antiquity, caused a beneficial increase in the difficulty of ascending to the highest through its attention to tests, ranks and bullying. It convinced people that the step they were on could not be a very high one, let alone the highest – through the mere fact that they were on it. In addition, the divine hierarchies offer considerable scope for ranks beyond human comprehension, which is why humans always have a motive to look upwards. They flourish only in the uncertainty of their admission to higher circles. Let us not forget that this mentality still informed Nietzsche's thinking when he sought to show his friends 'all the steps of the *Übermensch*.[6] Rainer Maria Rilke also showed his familiarity with the traditions of the upward glance when he invoked the 'pollen of the blossoming godhead, joints of light, hallways, stairs, thrones'.[7] It was only when the 'God-seeker gangs' of the nineteenth and twentieth centuries burst into this universe, built entirely on discretions, that the pathos of graded distance disappeared. The efforts of a world consisting of ranks, scales and ascents have since become incomprehensible to most people. Deregulated desire wants a 'flat hierarchy' – or even completely level ground. It no longer accepts any reason why it should not have everything on its own level immediately. Status and stasis evaporate here too – not, however, to force individuals to view their relationships with others through sober eyes,[8] but rather to leave them behind in a previously unknown state of defencelessness. In this condition they succumb first to the temptations of the extreme, then to those of a vulgarity without limits.

One could make similar observations in the case of prestige-laden negative theology. Its origins among the Greek church fathers, specifically the Cappadocians and Dionysius Pseudo-Areopagita, support the assumption that it was intended to mitigate the obsession with ascension in a spirit-metaphysically aroused monastic community of a Hellenistic-Christian variety. Though the educated among today's religion-lovers almost treat it like God's last intellectual chance, it actually served in its heyday as the ascetic's last chance to prevent spiritual infiltration by the frenzied masses. Its method was the slow pondering of lists consisting of concrete negations of the properties assigned to the Highest, whose constant

---

[6] Friedrich Nietzsche, *Thus Spoke Zarathustra* I, Zarathustra's Prologue, part 9.

[7] Rainer Maria Rilke, *Duino Elegies*, Elegy 2.

[8] 'All that is based on status and stasis evaporates, all that is holy is profaned, and humans are finally compelled to view their position in life and their relationships with others through sober eyes': Karl Marx and Friedrich Engels, *The Communist Manifesto*, part I.

repetition was meant to give meditators an awareness of their own distance from the pinnacle. Negative theology can only be productive as an intellectual litany that makes humans aware of the immeasurable distance between the unrecognizable God and his recognizable attributes. It cannot really be studied, only recited like a logical rosary. The exercise has the dual purpose of ensuring the transcendence of the super-objective object and coaxing the meditator away from the target area of deificatory frenzy. This satisfies the interest in polyvalence, as the faithful subject situates itself in a third position between a complete exclusion from God and a complete inclusion in him. As far as the modern use of this form of thinking is concerned, I shall restrict myself to observing that – as usual – the intention of those interested in it today is the opposite of the original exercise, as the highest can never be immanent and ego-near enough for them.

The various hermeneutical approaches stemming from an engagement with the Holy Scriptures can equally be considered schools of polyvalent thought behaviour. This is due primarily to the fact that professional scriptural exegetes are confronted with a dangerous alternative. The business of interpretation naturally calls for third options, as it is almost immediately faced with an unacceptable decision: either an excessively good or an excessively bad understanding of the divine message. Both options would have disastrous consequences. If one were to understand the scriptures as well as only their own author could, it would seem as if one wanted to clap God on the back and declare agreement with him – a claim that would hardly appeal to the guardians of holy traditions. If one's interpretation goes against the consensus, however, and in fact considers them completely opaque or nonsensical, it could be a case of demonic obstinacy. In both cases the recipient falls short of his duty, incurring the wrath of the orthodox establishment – which, as we know, was never squeamish when it came to laying down the law for heretics. Religious hermeneutics is thus located a priori in the space between two blasphemies and has to remain in limbo there. No situation could provide a better motive for committing oneself to a third option. If one cannot become one with the author's intentions as if one understood him better than he did himself at the moment of dictation, but is equally forbidden to miss his message as if he were some stranger with nothing to tell us, an escape to some middle ground is almost inevitable. The striving for a truthful understanding of the holy symbols is at home in the intermediate realm of interpretation, and its fundamental imperfection is its opportunity, its element. There is no need for any long-winded explanations of why such work, which takes place in the twilight of a meaning that is only ever partially revealed, has the strongest anti-extremist qualities – it can take its practitioners to the threshold between religious text and literature.[9] Paul Celan refers to the word's abstinence from oppressive authority when he states that poetry does not *im*pose, but rather *ex*poses itself.[10] In a conversation with Heiner Müller, who sometimes admitted that he no longer knew what he had meant in some line of his poetry, Alexander Kluge observed: 'You switch off your ears and pronounce verses.' This surely means that there is more sense in the world than the authors themselves can understand. The possibility of relaxing the hold of the absolute text in multiple readings has been most significant in the Jewish culture of commentary, whose richness stems from the

---

[9] The most resolute equation of holy text and poetry can be found in the writings of the American literary critic Harold Bloom, who has no qualms about comparing the God of the Yahwist with King Lear and Jesus with Hamlet. Cf. also Odo Marquard, *Abschied vom Prinzipiellen. Philosophische Studien* [Farewell to the Fundamental. Philosophical Studies] (Stuttgart: Reclam, 1981), pp. 127–32.

[10] Paul Celan, 'The Meridian. Speech on the Occasion of the Award of the Georg Büchner Prize' in *Selected Poems and Prose of Paul Celan*, trans. John Felstiner (New York and London: W. W. Norton, 2001), pp. 401–13.

proliferation of perspectives. Hence the profound jest: two Talmudic scholars, three opinions.

These effects are rounded off by the humour that develops in the shadow of the monotheisms. It shows a number of similarities with humour under dictatorships, as all totalizing systems, religious and political alike, provoke a popular backlash against the supposedly sublime that is forced on them. Humour can almost be considered the school for polyvalence, as it trains its apprentices to view every possible situation, in particular the more unpleasant ones, from a third perspective. This third view comes neither purely from below – from anxiety – nor purely from above – from indifference – but rather combines the upper and lower views in such a way that it has a liberating effect on the observer. Thus the subject can share in a more confident attitude towards its own situation. While philosophers have mostly used the motif of being superior to oneself in praise of self-control, humorists emphasize the aspect of self-therapy. In the context of cognitive theory, one would describe the practice of the third view as the reframing of a data mass in order to prevent consciousness from being overwhelmed by a paralyzing point of view. It is no coincidence that typical zealots instinctively recognize humour as the enemy that spoils business for the forces of militant one-sidedness. Wiser fighters compensate for their lack of humour with the assurance that laughter will be reserved for times of peace – just as Lenin considered it advisable to postpone listening to Beethoven's music until the fulfilment of Communism, as it seduces us into embracing our neighbour, even if he is a capitalist, instead of cracking his skull for the sake of a better future.

If one takes the effects of these disciplines as a whole, one can speak of civilization through institutionalization. For the participants of mature religious cultures, the good manners of informal polyvalence become second nature to such a degree that many passages from their own sacred texts which voice holy fury seem like embarrassing archaisms to them. In this predicament they resort to the discreetly heretical method of citing only those passages that are compatible with dominant sensibilities. A similarly selective approach to the whole text is also necessary among contemporary Catholics: it is not without reason that the controversial psalms of vengeance were recently removed from the Roman church's liturgy of the hours. The time will come when Muslims also decide to overlook the more sinister passages of the Qur'an. The civilizing process of the monotheisms will be complete once people are ashamed of certain statements made by their respective god and unfortunately documented, like the public appearances of a generally very amiable, but also irascible, grandfather who has not been allowed to mix with people without an escort for a long time.

7

The parables of the ring

Nowhere is the programme of a domestication of the monotheisms in the spirit of the good society evident more suggestively than in the parable of the ring from Lessing's 1779 dramatic poem *Nathan the Wise*. It tells the story of a father in the distant past who bequeathed a precious ring to his son. The ring possessed the magical ability to make its wearer agreeable to God and men, thus proving his identity as the legitimate heir. Following the model of this first handing-down, the ring wandered for a long time from each successive father to his son, regularly displaying its pleasing effects. In one generation, however, the owner of the ring had three sons who were all equally obedient and thus equally beloved, so that he promised the ring to each of them. The loving patriarch's virtuous weakness could only be balanced out by a virtuous deception: the old man had two imitations produced 'by an artist' that were of such perfection that not even he could tell the original apart from the two new rings. He then gave one to each of his sons with the appropriate blessings and promises.

After the father's death the inevitable happened: the sons began to quarrel, for each now staked his claim as the sole legitimate heir. The conflict was inescapable, but also irresolvable, for all three parties had equally valid reasons for their demands. A wise judge was called in to settle the matter. He found a solution by decreeing that all three should be put to the test. For this it was necessary to shift the focus from the level of religious claims and their proofs to the level of concrete effects. If 'the right ring can no longer be found' – and *eo ipso* the right faith, as Nathan emphatically adds – both the ring owners and their observers would have no choice but to submit to the pragmatic criterion. The power of the ring to 'make its wearer agreeable to God and men' would one day be the decisive factor. The candidates were left only with the advice to assist the inner virtues of the ring with their own efforts and 'sincere warmth'. Assessing the results would naturally have to wait until the distant future, when a further judge would summon the warring parties once again – an unmistakable allusion to an Enlightenment version of Judgement Day, on which not only individual believers, but the monotheistic religions as a whole would have to take responsibility for their actions.

From today's perspective, this parable, rightfully celebrated as the Enlightenment's equivalent of the Sermon on the Mount, shows its complete postmodernity: it combines primary pluralism, the positivization of simulation, the practical suspension of the question of truth, civilizatory scepticism, the shift from reasons to effects, and the priority of external approval over internal claims. Even the most hard-boiled reader cannot help admiring the wisdom of Lessing's solution: by postponing the final verdict until the end of time, it prevents the candidates for the truth from being sure of their selection. Thus Lessing's pious scepticism takes the religions seriously by giving them the hint not to take themselves too seriously.

It should not impair the venerability of the document if I note a few difficulties that complicate its seemingly straightforward meaning. What Lessing is suggesting amounts to a reception-aesthetic transformation of religion. This heralds the rise of mass culture in religious matters. In this context, 'Enlightenment' is no less than a codeword for the belief that the elite and the masses will one day, after overcoming their historically grown estrangement, come together in shared perceptions and value judgements. It was precisely this convergence that the young heroes of German Idealism invoked as a civilizatory opportunity on the way to their goal of doing away with 'the blind trembling of the people before its wise men and priests'.[1] 'And so the enlightened and the unenlightened must join hands, mythology must become philosophical and the people must become reasonable . . .'[2] If, however, the potential for popularity becomes a criterion for truth – and the mouthpiece of the elite clings to this demand *expressis verbis* – one can expect a shift of the competition between the religions to the humanitarian field: it is not for nothing that the religious taste of the masses has always been gratified by the spectacle of charity, assuming it does not make an excursion to the theatre of cruelty in the middle.

If one looks at the matter in the cold light of day, then, Lessing could have dispensed with the figure of the second arbiter who passes judgement in the distant future, for, since the Enlightenment, the trial of the religions has occurred not at the end of days, but rather as a daily plebiscite. This is expressed in the fluctuations of sympathy that have, since the early twentieth century, been ascertained through surveys. The prerequisite for this was that civil society itself, discreetly or indiscreetly, was declared a deity on earth.[3] Ironically enough, none of the

---

[1] G. W. F. Hegel, 'Ältestes Systemprogramm des deutschen Idealismus' [The Oldest System Programme of German Idealism] in *Werke in 20 Bänden*, vol. I: *Frühe Schriften* [Early Writings] (Frankfurt am Main: Suhrkamp, 1972), p. 236.
[2] Ibid.
[3] Cf. Niklas Luhmann, 'Grundwerte als Zivilreligion' [Basic Values as Civil Religion] in *Religion des Bürgers. Zivilreligion in Amerika und Europa* [The Religion of the Middle Class. Civil Religion in America and Europe], ed. Heinz Kleger and Alois Müller (Münster: LIT-Verlag, 2004), pp. 175–95.

monotheistic religions fares particularly well before the court of popular taste, as the criterion of effect does not usually act in their favour – it no longer requires great acumen, after all, to realize that there is a significant correlation between monotheism and unrest (or discomfort) in the world – and the possible popular forms of the monotheistic religions, as we shall see in a moment, are also a precarious affair. The meditative religions of the East, on the other hand, most prominently Buddhism, enjoy great popularity and respect – which does not, admittedly, tell us whether the sympathizers have any desire to become practising members of their preferred cults.

Thus Lessing and his source Boccaccio, from whose *Decameron* the story is taken (as the third tale of the first day), must face the question of whether they are on the right track in their interpretation of symbols. Could it not be that both have succumbed to an illusion in their depiction of the ring's effects? Let us recall: Lessing has his judge state that only the ring with the power to makes its wearer agreeable to God and men can be the genuine ring. Nathan himself emphasizes that if all three ring-owners were to prove agreeable only to themselves, they would all be 'deceived deceivers' – the liberality of the eighteenth century already permitted such things to be said. Only the one who gained the approval of his fellow humans would have plausible evidence of truly being on the right path. In fact, the duty of altruism has been inseparable from the classical religions ever since the surrender of the ego and the devotion to a great or small Other came to be considered the sign of true faith. That would mean that God alone could decide whether a believer is agreeable to him. Lessing, however, takes a risk – albeit one strongly supported by the zeitgeist – and expands the jury deciding the success of religion by including people in it. But who can guarantee that the quality of being agreeable to God is the same as that of garnering approval among humans?

In reality, no aspect expresses the essence of monotheism more succinctly than the willingness of the zealots to be hated by their fellow humans if that is how they can please God more. With his carefree equation of 'agreeable to God' and 'popular among people', Lessing was perhaps misled by early Enlightenment optimism, which took the convergence of elite and mass interests for granted as a natural result of progress. The actual development of modernity paints a completely different picture: it deepens the divide between high culture and mass culture with each new generation, making the hatred of high culture, or at least the majority's suspicion towards it, reveal itself ever more openly as a fundamental characteristic of recent events in civilization. If one draws the logical conclusions from this, one will understand why monotheism will one day be forced to lay its high-cultural cards on the table – and if it does not admit to its elitist streak, and indirectly also its polemogenic nature, it risks having others do so for it.[4]

The religion of the exclusive One must then admit, as if at the last minute, what it was never supposed to say openly: that it would go against its very nature to be popular. Any kind of popularity it enjoys stems from sentimental misunderstandings – the most famous example is Chateaubriand's rousing promotion of the 'genius of Christianity'. To him, the Romantic poet, even the strictest Catholic sacraments seemed like 'paintings full of poetry',[5] and he read the life stories of the saints as if they were the most fascinating novels. To balance out this idealized view, one should call to mind certain culture-historical principles: a monotheistic religion that defends the extent of its claims can only come to power and

---

[4] Cf. Jan Assmann, *Die Mosaische Unterscheidung oder Der Preis des Monotheismus* [The Mosaic Distinction or The Price of Monotheism] (Munich and Vienna: Hanser, 2003).
[5] Chateaubriand, *The Genius of Christianity or The Spirit and Beauty of the Christian Religion*.

remain in power by forcing the masses implacably to yield to its norms – which is impossible without a clerical dictatorship (usually under the patronage of a sacred or semi-sacred monarchy). In such an order of things, gentle and less gentle methods are equally in evidence. A regime of this kind was firmly established in Europe from the early Middle Ages to the eighteenth century – and it took long, extremely hard battles from the start of the Modern Age on to break the ubiquitous power of the church. Since then, the only way for both religious and aesthetic 'high culture' to reach the emancipated masses has been to switch to the mode of inner mission and dream of the golden age of mediaeval dominion.

The perspective of general cultural theory can help us to understand why the acceptance of monotheism by entire peoples and cultural circles has always required an extensive system of coercive methods. Once at the helm, a clericocracy stabilizes itself through the usual and inevitable 'culture-political' means: first and foremost, control of education[6] and an inquisitorial monitoring of orthodox obedience in all social strata. In addition to this, popular semi-Pagan compromises provide what is necessary to pacify the sensual needs of the masses. If high religion succeeds in converting the general antipathy towards them into rituals of admiration, this is the greatest possible achievement that lies within its means. A popular monotheism is a contradiction in terms.

In a corrected version of the ring parable, the father would have to order two completely identical new rings that would be tested practically for their power to make their wearer hated among people. Furthermore, the ring

---

[6] The civil religion of the French Revolution also sought to secure control of the hearts and minds of future generations. In his plans for republican institutions, Saint-Just wrote: 'Children belong to their mother until the fifth year of their lives, and from then until death they belong to the Republic.' Quoted in Friedrich Sieburg, *Robespierre the Incorruptible* (New York: Robert M. McBride, 1938).

should convey to its wearer the certainty of his election. The bearer of the magic symbol, however, will receive the confirmation of his special status at no extra charge: the antipathy of the many, who play their role more or less reluctantly in the comedy of admiration, will show him beyond doubt that he has chosen the right path. In this experiment, the monotheistic religions would be freed from any considerations of wanting to please one's fellow human beings – they could devote themselves unreservedly to their main project, i.e. being pleasing to the transcendent God alone. Each of the three would be at liberty to present itself as the most perfect form of personal supremacism; and if there were no way around a coexistence with the two other versions of the one-god-cult, each religion would at least be free to claim the crown of hatefulness for itself.

The history of the existing monotheisms fits unmistakably into a more clearly contoured picture if one takes this second version of the ring parable as its secret script. Behind the façade of a dispute over metaphysical truth, these religions have *de facto* waged a bitter contest of noble hatefulness – each one having the others as its audience, whose predictably negative reactions confirm their own respective successes. Admittedly, the ranking of the contestants has clearly fluctuated throughout history. While Judaism seemed for centuries to be the sure winner, and had to tolerate corresponding reactions on the part of the others, more recent history has seen dramatic changes of position – without a thorough examination of these, the spiritual and intellectual development of the West since the Renaissance is all but incomprehensible. When the Enlightenment thinkers of the eighteenth century turned their attention back to the fires of the holy inquisition and its learned instigators, Catholicism suddenly leapt far ahead: its apologists now seemed like shady characters, rising from the torture chambers of clerical absolutism and declaring terror the only way of forcing people towards salvation – one cannot help thinking of the figure of

Naphta from Thomas Mann's novel *The Magic Mountain*, who was intended to embody a satirical synthesis of Jesuitism and Communism. In the course of the twentieth century there was, surprisingly, another change at the forefront of the field. Islam, usually noted here only for its more violent expressions, had seemingly taken leadership overnight – which at least testifies to its undiminished capacity for provocation. It is now followed at some distance by Christianity, which gambled away its chances of taking the title of the most unpopular religion through the highly successful sympathy offensives of recent decades. Far behind the rest of today's field lies Judaism, which is almost being overwhelmed by hordes of admirers from all camps.

It can be said of all forms of zealotic monotheism that they are inconceivable without the figure of the scoffer, the one who rejects salvation and resolutely refuses to participate in its cults – in a word, the shadowy figure of the unbeliever. Such monotheism has thus shown two faces from the outset. It not only sets itself apart aggressively from all other cults, but also makes the rejection it encounters through its non-participants one of its driving motives – or more than that: it pragmatically assumes from the start that it will be unacceptable for many. To use one of Luhmann's phrases: it speculates on rejection. In order to reap its profits, it relies on the schema of exclusion through inclusivity: thanks to this, it can state with a clear conscience that it was never the one to turn others away – on the contrary, those people isolated themselves by refusing to participate. It shares this tactic with all avant-garde movements, which cannot possibly consider themselves at the vanguard without the majority lagging behind. In this sense, monotheism is only possible as a counter-religion in the first place, just as the avant-garde always constitutes a counter-culture. In fact, the development of a monotheistic position defined by the majority's resistance to it is constitutive, and without the constantly maintained awareness of the non-assimilable others, it would not be able to raise its internal tension to the necessary level. There can be no universalism without set-theoretical paradoxes: one can only invite everyone if one can be sure that not everyone will come.

The fully formed monotheistic cult stabilizes its metaphorical muscle tone by constantly reminding its followers of heresy within and the Pagan threat outside. Certainly it does not tire of invoking the virtue of humility before the Lord, but the sermon would be incomplete without the injunction that heathens and false teachers must be met with proud intransigence. If no real threat from without can be found, it can easily be replaced by imaginary sources of hatred. Without the daily state of emergency provoked by the temptations of the enemy, the high tension of religious life would rapidly decline into a state of ponderous non-aggression. Normally this field is characterized by the development of a two-enemy-economy that allows a back and forth between real and imaginary stressors. The highly current Islamic concept of a near and a remote enemy (in which the USA and Israel currently occupy the role of the external evil) is derived from this. Only Judaism managed largely without the devil, as it had the Egyptians and, after them, the Canaanites. These were followed by a long line of concrete oppressors, from the Babylonian kings to the German racists, who spared their victims the effort of merely imagining evil.

As a rule, however, one can always be sure of non-imaginary opponents, as the monotheistic provocation inevitably stirs a backlash among those provoked, sooner or later. There can be no Aten cult without the reaction of the Amun priesthood, no Judaism without the displeasure of the other peoples, no Christianity without the scepticism of the non-Christians, and no Islam without the unwillingness of the non-Muslims. Even in the early days of the Empire, educated Romans were so disturbed by the separatism of the Jews that they gave them the title 'enemies of the human race' (originally coined by Cicero to ostracize pirates). The young Hegel still noted, entirely conventionally: 'A people who spurns all other gods must carry the hatred of the entire human race in its heart.'[7] The two later monotheisms also provided their detractors with ample material for disapproval. In all cases, one can assume a co-evolution of thesis and antithesis. Here too, as is generally the case with over-determined and fed-back processes, reality seems to be dancing to the tune of the symbolic structure.

The consequences of these reflections for the trialogue of the monotheistic religions are obvious. At this point they need each other too much to fight any longer. In order to adjust from hostile coexistence to some kind of discussion, they must strike themselves from the list of 'hate providers', on which each has so far been the most important item for the others. This gesture is only conceivable on two conditions: either the moderately zealous monotheisms agree on a common foreign policy in relation to the non-monotheists – which would mean casting the role of the infidels with the indifferent (of which there is no lack in our times) in future, and replacing the heathens with the exponents of polytheisms, meditative cults and ethnic religions, whom one considers inferior from the outset. The advantage of this position for its defenders would be that of putting their rivalry on hold while still keeping universalist provocation alive: while shifting from mission to dialogue at the internal level, one could insist on expansion and spiritual priority at the external level.[8] Or, to posit the second condition, each monotheism can divest itself of the zealotic side of universalism and change into a non-zealous cultural religion – as has been the case

---

[7] Hegel, 'Entwürfe über Religion und Liebe' [Sketches on Religion and Love] (1797/8) in *Werke in 20 Bänden*, vol. I, p. 243.

[8] Elements of a similar historical compromise form the basis for the *entente cordiale* between Habermas and Ratzinger, which is only surprising to those who fail to see that present Catholicism and the civil-religiously committed second incarnation of Critical Theory cultivate the same bogeymen.

in liberal Judaism since the eighteenth century, in the great majority of Protestant churches since the nineteenth century, and in the liberal manifestations of Roman Catholicism since the Second Vatican Council. There have been analogous developments in Islam, especially in Turkey since 1924, but also in the Western diaspora, where it is always advisable to present oneself as capable of dialogue. This option demands no more than a transition from militant universalism to a civilized 'pretend' universalism – a tiny shift that makes all the difference. One can recognize the incorrigible zealots because they would carry out such a change tactically, but never out of genuine conviction; that would mean giving up the privilege of radicality that alone satisfies their pride. Those who remain zealous to the end would rather die than be simply one party among others.

When the path of civilization is the only one still open, the transformation of the zealotic collectives into parties must be put on the agenda. If one says 'parties', that automatically means a competition between them. Amidst such competition, the candidates must at least sacrifice their claims to universal dominance, if they are not going to stop believing in the superiority of their convictions. At the same time, exposing oneself to comparisons implies an admission that human standards are binding at their own level. It is inevitable that the popularity criteria of everyday humanity will also apply once more, and – why not? – the rules of play in a mass culture fluctuating between sentimentality and cruelty. It is one thing to strive to please the zealous God; it is another matter when one is dealing with a rediscovered necessity to please the common people in spite of everything, always bearing in mind that zealous monotheisms are not generally to their taste.

This takes us back to the ring parable in its original version. On our excursion into the secret history of unpopularity, we have discovered motives to find out more precisely who that wise judge who finally assesses the results of the competition might be – a contest that will turn out to have been a double fight for both popularity and hatefulness. Lessing's information that the final test will be taken 'after one thousand times one thousand years' removes any reasonable doubt that he is thinking of a large-scale world trial. This would involve not only the apocalypse of guilty souls, but also a final judgement of the guilty religions. Although Lessing's first referee speaks discreetly of a future colleague who would have to know much more than he does – which seems to point to a human – it is absolutely clear that the figure of the second judge is intended to be equated with God. What God is he then referring to? Can the second judge in the ring parable really be the God of Abraham, who was supposedly also the God of Moses, the duo of Jesus and Paul, and the prophet Mohammed? It must be permissible to doubt these identities in both directions – retrospectively, because equating Abraham's El with the YHWH of the Mosaic religion, the father of the Christian trinity and Mohammed's Allah cannot be more than a pious convention, or rather an echo effect that appears beneath the resonating domes of religious semantics – and prospectively, because the entire history of religion proves that, even within monotheistic traditions, the later God retains only a very slight resemblance to the God of the early days.

This makes it uncertain whether God the judge can still be the ally of his earliest zealots at the moment of the final trial. Has he himself remained the zealous and jealous God? In the end, his benevolence towards his earlier partisans can no longer be unquestioningly assumed, as he has clearly moved beyond an immaturely wrathful phase. At the most, he would acknowledge extenuating circumstances – for his followers, and via this detour also for himself – by pardoning their zealotry as a transitional neurosis that served an evolutionary purpose. The first exponents of zealous mono-truth may genuinely have had legitimate motives for snubbing their fellow humans and burdening them with a fundamental opposition in the name of the totally other. For the cultural historian, it is certainly understandable why primitive monotheism had to attack both the natural and the cultural thusness of humans. Its task was to destroy their overly self-assured rooting in lineage, their trust in the world and love of images, and their life in a state of moral approximation, in order to confront them directly with the steep wall of the law. It is at this wall that the worldling nature fails – and it is supposed to, for the holy warriors firmly believe that worldly self-satisfaction as a whole must be destroyed. For any true zealot it is evident that humans can only be heathens at first, and forever if one leaves them alone – *anima naturaliter pagana*. Without a collision with the 'true God' and his demanding messenger, the most they will ever achieve are splendid vices. Hence one must never leave them alone, and should interrupt their habits whenever possible. As pre-monotheistic habits somehow always happen to be bad ones, the re-education of the human race became the order of the day after the monotheistic caesura. Then the following dictum applies: 'The Lord disciplines those he loves' (Proverbs 3:12 and Hebrews 12:6). Hegel still referred to this as 'the higher standpoint that man is evil by nature, and evil because he is natural'.[9] Without the punitive resistance of the law, known in other contexts as the 'symbolic order', humans cannot, in the view of their monotheistic disciplinarians, become what they are supposed to. Robespierre's trend-setting dictum 'whoever trembles is guilty' is still very much in the spirit of this sublime pedagogy, where punishment is considered the honour of the blasphemer. In a

---

[9] Hegel, *Vorlesungen über die Philosophie der Religion II. Vorlesungen über die Beweise vom Dasein Gottes* [Lectures on the Philosophy of Religion II. Lectures on the Proofs of God's Existence] in *Werke in 20 Bänden*, vol. XVII, section entitled 'Die Bestimmung des Menschen' [The Destiny of Man], p. 253.

related sense, Kierkegaard would later instruct his readers that whoever wishes humans well must place obstacles in their path.

Everything else transpires from the duty of scandal. One has to admit that the followers of the One God have not made things easy for themselves in this respect. The offending peoples, the chosen, the baptized, the militant and, last but not least, the analysed, carried the burden of their task along with them and undertook the daring, but thankless, business of advancing spiritualization by unpopular methods. In their eyes, humans are creatures to whom one can only do justice by overtaxing them. They are creatures that only come to their senses when one demands more of them than simply what is customary among speaking apes.

Then, however, something happened that no old-style zealot could have reckoned with: once provoked, people suddenly began to learn more quickly than their provocateurs had believed possible. The European Renaissance marked the start of a cycle of new examinations of God and the world that points beyond the historical monotheisms. The thinkers of the century after the Reformation discovered the general of which monotheism was the particular. What we call the Enlightenment was, from a religion-historical perspective, no more or less than a rupture of the symbolic shells that had imprisoned the historical style of zealous universalisms. To put it as paradoxically as it appears: with its growing self-assurance, the Enlightenment not only broke away from the historically developed monotheisms; it in fact produced a higher-level monotheism in which various universal articles of faith attained dogmatic validity. These include the a-priori unity of the species, the indispensability of the state under the rule of law, the destiny of humans to control nature, solidarity with the disadvantaged and the disabling of natural selection for *Homo sapiens*. 'Enlightenment' is simply the popular name for the perpetual literary council in which these articles are discussed, fixed and defended against heretics.

Anyone looking for the prototype of the resulting fundamentalism will find it in Rousseau's sketch of a *religion civile* as expounded in his text on the social contract from 1758. It provided the most rigorous neo-monotheism with form and content – and its consequences were much more far-reaching than any of the first Enlightenment thinkers could have foreseen. Its formulation constituted an admission that even post-Christian 'society' must be rooted in certain human moral intuitions. Whoever uses the world 'society' is implicitly also saying 'social religion'. When Napoleon Bonaparte returned to Catholicism as the French state religion following the anti-Catholic excesses of the revolution, he *de facto* declared it the new civil religion, thus subjecting the 'substantial truth of faith' to an incurable functional irony. Since then, Christianity itself has been the substitute religion for Christianity.

But that was not all. In keeping with its highly active nature, the Enlightenment prepared its transition to post-monotheistic positions. It was inevitable that it would strike the item 'God' from its budget and fill the resulting vacancy with the 'human being'. Even when it pushed ahead to atheism, however, its structure initially remained a copy of the monotheistic projects. Consequently it released an immanent zealotry that – because it was incapable of grace – even surpassed the religious variety in strictness, anger and violence. This escalation of fury for the greatest of human causes is what is meant when people refer to the historical sequence extending from Jacobin rule to the frenzy of Maoism as the age of ideologies. Ideologies in the strong sense of the word are movements that ape the form of zealous monotheism with atheistic world projects.

This enlightened para-monotheism set itself apart critically from the historical religions by revealing the general quality present in all concepts of God that conformed to the personal-supremacist type: the new movement undoubtedly argued most convincingly when it pointed to the fact that every one of the historical monotheisms was based on projections, and thus still constituted a cult of images: they invite people to enter into an imaginarily determined relationship with the Highest – even, and in fact especially, in cases where the absence of images in dealings with the supreme being had been of the utmost importance. In this sense Marx was right to claim that all critique is based on the critique of religion. The projective quality of the concept of God in the sphere of the subjectivist supremacisms is evident in the elementary observation that God, in spite of all bans on representation, is consistently understood as a person and addressed as the Lord. It is precisely the aniconic religions based on an avoidance of images, namely Judaism and Islam, that seem like bastions of the most tenacious idolatry from this perspective. Just as Malevich's *Black Square* remains a picture even as a non-picture, the Black Person of monotheistic theologies is still a portrait as a non-portrait, and an idol even as a non-idol.

It is more important now than ever to beware of psychology, which tends to attribute even the greatest projects to small mechanisms in those carrying out the projection. In its view, the smaller element reveals the truth about the greater one. Monotheistic projects, on the other hand, express the fact that people, whether they like it or not, are inevitably always in a state of vertical tension. They not only want to elevate themselves to something greater, even the greatest; they are also enlisted, through spiritual experiences and evolutionary challenges, to assist events taking place on a higher level. Thus projects of this type exert an upward pull on humans, which is why they are damned to be superior to themselves (as Socrates explains in Plato's *Republic*) – even if they often do not know how to deal with this superiority.

The statement 'man infinitely transcends man' was already a product of the crisis that revealed the general aspect of the historical monotheisms. As soon as its principle was formulated with sufficient clarity, it could be detached from its traditional forms. From that point, further modification of the monotheistic programmes became the business of extra-religious agencies: one half of the formulating work was taken over by great politics, the other by great art. Now it was possible for people to come along and declare that politics is destiny – while others claimed the same for art. Since the dawn of Romanticism, great art has meant a transferral of the provocation of humans to the eminent work by means of the law. Since the American Revolution, great politics has meant the entrance of monotheism into the age of its artificial stageability.

In its deep structure, Lessing's tale of indistinguishable copies is speaking about these very transitions. The story of the two duplicate rings does not simply contain the message that even wonderful things are artificially produced; it also communicates in a fairly blunt fashion that the question of authenticity is rendered trivial by the interest in effects. Only incorrigible fetishists are still interested in originals and proofs of origin. In the world of currentness, however, effects are all that matter.

I now feel compelled to present a third version of the ring parable, despite having just returned to the original, where everyday human judgement is one of the decisive factors in the evaluation of the religions. This additional correction will now give the zealous party another chance to be heard. This time the people in question are zealots who fight against humanity for the sake of humanity – or to put it more precisely: in the name of the true human being of the future against the historically developed, misguided human being.

In this latest revision of the parable we hear of the production of a fourth ring, symbolizing a political atheism that will stop at nothing. This atheism claims it is fulfilling the truth of the three monotheisms by transferring them back to earth from heaven. It appears under the name of Communism, whose root *communio* evokes the synthesis of past peoples of God – Israel, the church and the *ummah*. The term itself implicitly expresses the new political universalism's objection to the historical folk traditions, which, from the perspective of avant-garde morality, merit only contempt: only people who are too stupid to become general producers, i.e. true human beings, carry their communal membership around with them like the flag of an organization. Similar ideas had been anticipated by Christianity and Islam. The new faith went further, propagating the thesis that it had shown the valid basis for every membership in God's community that was still possible among humans, with the international industrial proletariat at its centre as its miserable and creative elite. Consistently enough, Communism could – for a while – claim the advantage of being the ring that was far more than simply an identical replica of earlier rings. Its production could only be undertaken once interest in the older rings had begun to diminish due to new insights and the accompanying new hopes.

This brings us to Communism's strongest argument, which, when explicitly laid out, leads to the fiery centre of modern thought. Whoever acknowledges the possibility of fundamentally new insights is admitting something that older historical metaphysics would not have accepted at any price: that truth itself is subject to evolution, and that the succession of events is more than simply a random sequence. It is in the nature of truth itself that it cannot be fully revealed from the start, but rather comes to light consecutively, bit by bit, as a cumulatively developed result of investigations that may never reach an end.

This reflection leads to a new definition of the sense of the revealed religions: holy scriptures of this type can only be legitimated as catastrophic interruptions or extreme accelerations of human research history. By supporting its case with the claim of a divine intervention in the investigations of humans, each becomes an organ of holy impatience. They express the sentiment that the truth is too important to wait for the research to be completed. As time-honoured as these religions may seem to us today, they are all early comers by nature; they set faith the tasks that the science of the time could not handle by itself.

The term 'revelation' itself makes this prematurity clear, as it contains a statement about the condition of human spirituality: it must show an adequate level of development to be receptive to a revelation of the monotheistic variety, but should still be in a sufficiently undeveloped state to require help from above. Indeed, all revelations would be superfluous if they did not convey something that the human spirit could not access on its own strength in the respective status quo. It is in this 'not yet' quality that the whole significance of the revealed religions lies. What they have in common is their quasi-putschist determination to break out of the openness of a life full of experimentation in order to jump ahead to the end of all attempts and errors. In terms of their status in the world process, the historical monotheisms can be understood as petrified interjections in the continuing sequence of experiences where experiment and apocalypse coincide. They draw their authority from the certainty with which they claim to be speaking from the perspective of the true end. They embody the attempt to anticipate, in the middle of the world experiment, the result of everything that can ever be achieved in a learning life – at least, in moral and eschatological terms. Their existence stands or falls with this risk; it is their sole source of legitimacy.

Thus the revealed religions tend not only towards a devaluation of everything so far understood and achieved to a more or less useless prelude – this is the purpose of their sometimes fanatical anti-Pagan polemic (whose exaggerations later have to be corrected through retroactive retrievals of something supposedly devalued, but in fact often superior and indispensable – one need only think of Greek philosophy and the results of the pre-Christian and pre-Islamic sciences) – but additionally deny the possibility and inevitability of finding new truths, if these happen to produce results leading to revisions in the text of the holy scriptures. Such religions, as noted above, can therefore only be understood as vehicles of hastiness; and their evaluation hangs by the thread of how far it can be shown that there are anticipations which resist all attempts at revision – and that such anticipations form their substance. If there is a convincing justification for the theological profession in all religions, it is presumably only through an explanation of their true activity: it is their job to prevent the revelations from being rendered obsolete through later, newer events by constantly showing anew the undiminished currentness of aspects that are seemingly outdated. Only if the religious scholars can show plausibly how the holy texts in fact contain leaps into the realm of the absolutely final that one can partially catch up with, but never overtake, will they be able to assert their claims to truth.

This reflection leads to a slightly more technical reinterpretation of the concept of revelation. A reformulated notion of revelation provides an explicit basis for the relationship between what is revealed and the ongoing learning period of intelligent collectives. In process-logical terms, revelation means the elevation of a prejudgement to a final judgement. It combines a symbol from the relative sphere with the level of the absolute. Such an operation makes it necessary to replace the classical concept of eternity with that of absolute velocity. The term 'revelation' hence implies an acceleration of insight to absolute velocity. It postulates the synchronization of human insight with the transrapid intelligence of God. Only through this can prejudgements and final judgements coincide. A holy scripture would then simply be a vessel for conclusive and trustworthy statements through which all insights taking place at relative velocities would be overtaken. Even in so eminent a text, however, the few unovertakeable statements will inevitably be surrounded by numerous others that can potentially be overtaken or have in fact been overtaken. The margin of difference between the strong and weak statements in a sacred body of text makes room for ways of adapting faith to the respective day and age.

Against this background, we can explain the philosophical meaning of the project known as Communism once again. In accordance with its dogmatic quality, it consisted in an abrogation of all earlier prophetic statements and their reformulation in a language of realism, where the latter was conceived in a dual sense – both as economic production, a metabolic exchange between humans and nature, and as political practice, as an appropriation of the humanly possible by real human beings. The expressions 'real human being' and 'revolutionary' now become synonymous. That would mean the baton of prophetism was handed from Moses to Jesus, from Jesus to Mohammed, and from Mohammed to Marx. Marx would have rejected the religious narrowness of his predecessors and sought to put an end to all mystified forms of revelation. He would have placed the truths of the religions on trial before the worldly sciences and proletarian passions. He would, like any fair judge, have allowed them to act as the 'soul of a heartless world', but nonetheless rejected the majority of their statements in order to replace them with a political practice that acted in favour of real human beings.

The fourth ring, then, can only indirectly be compared to the older ones. At most, one could say that the other three were melted down for its fabrication in order to take the best qualities from the moral substance of each. Its claim to superior validity is based on the thesis that its production no longer takes place under the law of religious projection, but rather due to an insight into the productive nature of humans. The prophet of the fourth ring postulated a world in which all people would become free producers of their own destiny, both as individuals and collectively.

It was precisely this expectation that had to remain essentially unfulfilled in the spheres of activity of the religions that have existed so far, as they always involved classes of people, the ones known as rulers, who prevented the vast majority of others, those known as the oppressed and exploited, from freely producing and appropriating their own selves. Ironically enough, the clerics of the three-ring religions, especially the extremely feudalized high clergy in Christianity, were also among the oppressed classes, which meant that one could not expect any direct help from them in reaching the goal of general emancipation. Is that not why the Protestant Reformation revolted against the arrogance of the ruling Roman church? Did the theologian Martin Dibelius not see valid reasons, even in the middle of the twentieth century, to refer to the church as the 'bodyguard of despotism and capitalism'? Understandably, depriving the exploitative clergy of its power must be declared a fundamental prerequisite for the realization of those prophecies through which the wearers of the fourth ring sought to make themselves agreeable to their fellow humans. In order to establish this 'religion of man' (to apply a phrase of Rousseau's reference to Communism), however, it became inevitable that the pleasant would be preceded by the terrible. Only one thing was certain for the zealots of humanity: as long as the lords of the older rings exercised their power over people's souls, human beings would not infinitely transcend the human, but rather fall infinitely short of themselves.

The Communists worked consistently on the development of an anthropological supremacism of a resolutely anti-religious character. In this undertaking it was allowed – in fact necessary – to blaspheme the imaginary Highest in the name of the real highest. Each effective blasphemy meant an overstepping of the 'existing' towards liberating excess. This is the meaning of the 'passion for the real' (*passion du réel*), which, according to a shrewd observation by Alain Badiou, was the hallmark of the twentieth century.[10] In the parlance of the zealots of humanity, the movement through which human beings with a low standing could potentially attain the level of the highest human being was known as 'revolution'. Because revolution constituted a translation of revelation into political practice, however, it shared its risk of excessive haste. It too, while still caught up in the experiment of creating wealth, ignored the question of whether the conditions were right and the means sufficiently tested and sought to force results that would be impossible to overtake at later stages of the world's development.

The rest of the story is well known. Within a few generations, after some successful conversions at the start, the fourth ring made its wearer the object of almost unconditional disgust without giving him any chance to make himself agreeable to God as a compensation. The hatefulness of what was done in the name of Communism was demonstrated to the extreme for judgement by all normal humans – and if one still occasionally encounters the opinion that the atrocities committed on the other side surpassed those of Communism, it is primarily because those in the corresponding circles refuse to accept the facts: with over 100 million lost lives, the degree of human extermination achieved in Communist systems is several times higher than that of Hitler's regime, which has – understandably – been given the title of absolute evil. The question arises whether a co-absolute evil should not have been added to the collective consciousness long ago.

---

[10] Alain Badiou, *Century*, trans. Alberto Toscano (Cambridge: Polity Press, 2007 [original edition published in 2005]). The author weakens his case through grotesque errors of judgement, however, for example when he adopts the attitude of an unrepentant revolutionary priest and defends the mass killings instigated by Stalin and Mao. For a partial response to Badiou's book, cf. Peter Sloterdijk, 'Was geschah im 20. Jahrhundert? Unterwegs zu einer Kritik der extremistischen Vernunft' [What Happened in the Twentieth Century? Towards a Critique of Extremist Reason], lecture given in Strasbourg on 3 March 2005.

For the majority of people at that time, it remained unclear to what extent the Soviet and Chinese dramas constituted a parody of religious history since the caesura on Mount Sinai. Moses' command 'let every man kill his brother, his friend and his neighbour' was obviously only followed on a grand scale by the ideologues of humanity in the twentieth century; one had to wait until the advent of monohumanism to witness the hubristic seeds of monotheism bloom. The lesson of this unprecedented episode would prove difficult to forget: if it is already precarious to make people feel enthusiasm for a God who demands too much of them, even if it is to their own advantage, then it is completely impossible to turn people into zealots of humanity beyond brief moments of hysteria – least of all by the methods with which the Russian and Chinese Communists sought to achieve their goals.

This brings us back to the original version of the ring parable a second time, and this time – if we are not very much mistaken – we shall stick to it once and for all. In the post-Communist situation, people began to understand that they could not avoid participating as jurors in the evaluation of the general religions and their political derivations. In the light of the catastrophe of Communism, it became necessary to pronounce judgement in the middle of the process, and the assessment of the zealots of humanity – like those of revelation and revolution – will inevitably run the risk of prematurity. The jury's verdict leaves no room for doubt: it abrogates the revolution, which was a step backwards, and chooses the lesser evils, namely the liberal state under the rule of law, democracy and capitalism. It is clear that this does not necessarily constitute any final, binding result; but this intermediate status is significant in itself. As soon as one accepts its validity, the process that will pave the way for any possible inhabitable future can, in the shadow of past excesses, begin once more: that of civilizatory learning towards an existence of all human beings characterized by the universally imposed necessity of sharing a single planet.[11]

As the rejection of the principles, methods and results of Communism reached a high level of general validity – aside from isolated cases of malign incorrigibility – the jurors could once more turn their attention to the project of civilizing humanity, which had lost momentum through the various instances of totalitarian haste. At the same time, it becomes evident to what extent the relative slowness and apparent triviality of the secular world design increase the general dissatisfaction within civilization. This provides the conventional religions with new recruits. More than a few of yesterday's protagonists who are now on the rise once again are noting with satisfaction that the days are past when it was thought that a critique of religion was the precondition for all critique. They relish the atmosphere in which the cessation of a critique of religion seems to be paving the way for the end of all critique.

This necessitates a sensitive distinction. If the historical religions have been improving their reputations again in certain respects, there are two completely different reasons for this, and their respective legitimacy runs very deep, even though they are mutually exclusive – I do not wish to say whether temporarily or permanently so. For

---

[11] Cf. Bruno Latour, 'La Terre est enfin ronde' [In the End, the Earth is Round] in *Libération*, 1 February 2007, p. 28, where the author takes up a word I have suggested, 'monogëism', and uses it to formulate a principle of reality for the global age. 'Monogëism' is a semi-satirical expression intended to point to both the premise and the result of terrestrial globalization, the nautical occupation of the earth by the Europeans. (Cf. [Sloterdijk] *Im Weltinnenraum des Kapitals*, p. 252.) Without the seafarers' faith in a navigable earth, the world in its modern system could not have been established. The expression states that the mere fact of the number one is absolutely binding with reference to the earth, while remaining problematic with reference to God – whose numerical value fluctuates between zero and one, even extending to three and the symbol for many. This means that, compared to monotheism, monogëism constitutes a more stable cognitive object.

the first group of interested parties, both traditional and synthesized religion are now once more – and will continue to be – what they have always been: a medium of self-care and a participation in a more general or higher life (functionally speaking: a programme for stabilizing the personal and regional-collective immune system by symbolic means). For the second circle, religion remains the guardian of unresolved moral provocations designed to develop each ordinary member of the species into the 'general human being' – though one should bear in mind that such classifications as Jew, Christian, Muslim, Communist or *Übermensch* offer partly problematic and partly false names for the 'general human being' (I shall leave aside the question of whether the 'general human being' is itself a problematic or false name for the existential form of the competent individual in 'world society').

The post-Communist situation holds opportunities for both sides: for the members of the first group, because they can attend once more – undisturbed by the total influence of other collectives – to their personal integration, or, in more technical words: the regulation of their psychosemantic constitution; and for the members of the second group, because they are now free to pursue, under different conditions, the question of whether there might be a less hasty way to generalize forces of human freedom. One could also frame the riddle in the following terms: has Communism left behind a secret last will that still remains to be found and opened by subsequent generations?[12] In fact, the problem associated here with the fourth ring continues to be the great mystery of our time. The production of the 'general human being' through the politics of haste undoubtedly failed; but this does not in any way make its opposite, namely a merely vital existence shrunken down to its bare minimum among people in the despiritualized zones of prosperity, acceptable. The

---

[12] Boris Groys, *Das kommunistische Postskriptum* (Frankfurt am Main: Suhrkamp, 2006).

new interest in the great religions can be attributed primarily to the fact that, since the self-renunciation of Communist and Socialist humanity politics, the traditional religious codes have been all that is available when people look for more comprehensive forms of communal consciousness – at least, for as long as there are no transculturally convincing formulations of a general theory of culture on offer.

We should note: the jury deciding on the success of the zealous religions is forced to accept in the course of its work that there is a grave lack of criteria for evaluating the exclusive universalisms, whether religious or worldly in their coding. In this way a programme of making all content explicit becomes the order of the day, enlisting the services of philosophy, theology, religious science and, above all, cultural theory. If it applies that people in the current phase of civilization are faced with the difficulty of having to reach temporarily final judgements on temporarily final results of historical learning, including the shortcuts to eternity that exist in the form of the revealed religions, one should at least facilitate the task through aids to judgement that correspond to the current state of art.

Owing to a malicious dialectic, these facilitating factors seem like hindrances. One can at least hold onto the initial assumption that intellectual and spiritual tools such as Euclidean geometry, Aristotelian logic, the Ten Commandments and fasting in the month of Ramadan, which have endured millennia, contain something that, for better or for worse, can be considered final. As modules of truth for simple logical and moral situations, these norms cannot be overtaken. In a different sense, however, they have been constantly overtaken for some time – certainly not through simple disablement, but rather in the mode of integrating elementary aspects into more complex patterns. The development of non-Euclidean geometries, non-Aristotelian systems of logic and non-decalogical moralities shows clearly in what ways the world can still learn. Another item on this list would be non-Ramadanic dietary science, a discipline through which Muslim women in Turkey and elsewhere learn how to avoid the almost inescapable gain in weight resulting from the opulent feasts after sunset during the fasting month.

8

After-zeal[1]

Following the collapse of Communism, the question of monotheism remained unresolved. Instead of leaving it behind, forgotten, the implosion of the movement treated here as the fourth manifestation of militant universalism in fact redirected attention to the historical monotheisms – which, more or less discreetly, used the situation to their advantage. At the same time, it laid the foundations for a new series of religion-critical investigations whose significance has gone largely unnoticed by the wider audience. These provide a contrast to the ubiquitous theories about the 'return of religion'. They also address once more (following the interrupted attempts at a critique of fanaticism in the eighteenth century) the polemogenic effects of monotheistic zealotry, the intolerance and hatred of otherness as such, with a suitably fundamental and comprehensive approach. The gravity of the debate stems from the now widely justified suspicion that the acts of violence carried out by the followers of Christianity and Islam were not mere distortions, falsifications of the true nature of essentially benign religious doctrines, but rather

---

[1] Translator's note: the original title 'Nach-Eifer' suggests a play on words. While the hyphenation sets it apart from the verb *nacheifern*, meaning 'to emulate', the choice of words implies that both a post-zealotic state and certain examples of emulation are meant here.

manifestations of a polemogenic potential that is inseparable from their existence.

In this situation, the cultural sciences are attracting attention once again. With his sensational books *Moses der Ägypter* and *Die mosaische Unterscheidung*,[2] the Egyptologist Jan Assmann not only initiated a vigorous world-wide debate on the psychohistorical costs of monopolistic claims to truth in post-Mosaic religious developments, but also provided general religious and cultural science with a new, hermeneutically powerful concept in the form of his idea of 'counter-religion'. But it seems that Assmann, in keeping with the idiosyncratic nature of his themes, only connected a part of his term's possible semantic content to the present. First he presents the monotheistic Aten cult, founded in the fourteenth century BC by the Pharaoh Akhenaten, as the first example of an explicit counter-religion; then he advances and supports the fascinating argument that this episodic prototype was followed, in the form of Mosaic monotheism, by the first model of a counter-religion that stood the test of time – at a high price for its carrier people, as we know. It is in the elusive nature of the subject that the connections between the Akhenatic prelude and the act of Moses cannot be disentangled entirely. In order to shed more light on them, cultural science must show its worth as the art of indirect proof and operate in a twilight zone between histories of effect, motive and memory. Particular complications arise from the chronological circumstances, which now make it difficult to endorse wholeheartedly Sigmund Freud's speculative identification of Moses with a priest of the Aten religion. The virtuosity with which Assmann carried out his task made no small contribution to sensitizing contemporary reflections on the stability of

---

[2] Jan Assmann, *Moses the Egyptian. The Memory of Egypt in Western Monotheism* (Cambridge, Mass.: Harvard University Press, 1997), as well as *Die Mosaische Unterscheidung oder Der Preis des Monotheismus.*

different cultures anew to the questions raised by political theology.

The high level of argumentation and the variety of perspectives evident in the answers provoked by Assmann's venture convey a clear message. They prove no less than the fact that the disciplines of ancient history are in the process of regaining the culture-political pathos lost since the decline of the humanist educational paradigm and the marginalization of classical studies after 1945. While the European battle of cultures known as the Renaissance, however, which lasted from the fifteenth to the twentieth centuries, was fought mainly on the front between returning Greek culture and fading Christian culture, it is an older, more radical and more complicated front between Egyptian and Jewish culture that is becoming visible once more today.

Assmann's intervention describes and supports a paradigm shift that led to a change of emphasis from a Hellenocentric to an Egyptocentric renaissance. As a renaissance constitutes a polemical form of cultural comparison that takes place not only in the fields of philology, epistemology and art, but also, and especially, as a competition between the old and new schools of theology, it is quite understandable if such a declared 'rebirth' creates a very strong critical tension. A phenomenon of this kind can only ever assert its own value at the expense of the host cultures. The idea of something old being reborn implies a demand for a right of return for exiled and forgotten ideas, arts and virtues – a right that can only be asserted and granted if the later culture's claim to being more complete in every respect can be challenged with convincing arguments. This occurred in exemplary fashion in fourteenth-century Europe, when philologists, artists, engineers and scientists of the burgeoning Modern Age united to defend the right of the Greek scientific cultures and arts to be renewed against the inadequacies of Christian world knowledge and artistic skill. The partisanship of innumerable scholars and artists for the ancient ideas' right of return resulted in the civilization of modern Europe, which owes its wealth primarily to its bipolar disposition as a dual culture based on Judeo-Christian and Hellenic-humanist sources.

In analogy to the events beginning in fourteenth-century Europe, we must ask today whether the conditions are given for an import of ideas from an even more remote antiquity, and, if so, what these are. One would have to establish to what extent Egyptian motifs would be considered significant – as Assmann suggests with his liberal ethical flair and comprehensive erudition. In order to answer this question, we must examine the concept of counter-religion and its still only partly explored consequences. Even in Assmann's argumentation, it does not simply serve as an ad hoc characterization of the caesura that suddenly imposed itself on the world of ancient polytheisms – first through the Akhenaten disaster, then through Mosaic Judaism. Rather, it identifies a historically influential type of polemically zealotic religions whose effects are still making their partly beneficial, partly destructive virulence felt today. An evaluation of these is indispensable if one wishes to investigate whether an authentic Renaissance motif actually supports the older religious formations abolished by the counter-religions.

In this context we shall now shift our attention from the anti-Egyptian, anti-Canaanite and anti-Babylonian counter-religion of the Jews to the multiple counter-religion of the Christians, which combined anti-Roman, anti-Hellenic, anti-Jewish and anti-Pagan qualities. It will also be directed at the counter-religion of the Muslims, which primarily unified anti-polytheistic, but also partly anti-Christian and anti-Jewish motifs of protest. In addition, the bourgeois Enlightenment of the eighteenth century, specifically in the zealotic strands of the French Revolution with their totalitarian cult of reason and virtue, displayed unmistakably counter-religious traits, in some cases with a fanatical, anti-Catholic and anti-feudal direction. Nor is there any doubt that the militant atheism of the Communist movement showed all the hallmarks of a zealotic counter-religion based on a rejection of most previous cultural traditions. It was above all the 'bourgeoisie' that now became the heathendom of Communism. Even the fascist movements episodically presented themselves as nationalist-apocalyptic counter-religions, with an anti-Semitic, anti-Christian and anti-capitalist zealotry setting the tone. This means that substantial parts of occidental religious and intellectual history were commensurate with the campaigns of the counter-religions, whose cross-party banner is always found in that combination of combativeness and claim to truth which naturally stimulates intolerance.

I think that the problem I am, following Assmann's suggestions, hinting at here, with the catchword of a renaissance under the sign of Egypt, is sufficiently clearly defined for a provisional understanding. It implies a cultural comparison in which the cultures of intolerance in the Middle East and Europe would have to deal with the right of return of a forgotten and suppressed culture of tolerance of an Egyptian (potentially also a Mediterranean or Indian) type – not only in ethical terms, but also at the level of ontology and cosmology. Assmann has suggested the expression 'cosmotheism' for this complex that is capable of a virtual renaissance (or at least needs to be remembered). It denotes a religious world design that, owing to its internal qualities, especially the principle of multiple representations of the Highest, prevents the inception of one-sided zealotic reductions.

Naturally it would be unfounded to speak of a rebirth of the Egyptian gods today, either literally or metaphorically – in any case, the necessary conditions for the conceptual and experiential form of world-godliness are no longer given. On the whole, a serious return to polytheistic standards in the ancient style is not on anyone's agenda. What could develop under the heading of 'Egypt', however, is an active remembrance of a lighter religious climate in which the poison of declarations of enmity towards alternative cults, in particular the image-worshipping religions, had not yet filtered through to the rest of society.

One could very reasonably voice the objection that what I have here described as an Egyptocentric renaissance has, in fact, long since taken place. And indeed, the rebirth of antiquity among Europeans has not stopped at the revival of Greek and Roman patterns. Almost from the start, Egyptian paradigms also attracted the attention of European scholars, who had wanted to learn a second language to meet their metaphysical needs since the end of the Middle Ages. Their fascination with the Nile culture reached such a high level that no cultural history of the Modern Age was considered complete without an appropriately detailed consideration of the universe of hieroglyphophiles, Egyptosophers and Pharaonomaniacs. The Masonic Enlightenment in particular often fell back on Egyptian motifs to satisfy its need for symbols, which it used to flesh out a post-Christian religion of reason and tolerance.[3] The decisive aspect of these re-animations was not their exotic decor, but rather the prospect of an old-new paradigm of wisdom that would destroy the foundations for religious fanaticism of an exclusive monotheistic variety.

Ironically enough, the pinnacle of the liberal and cosmophile renaissance manifested itself in neither the language of Egypticism nor that of Hellenism. It was Friedrich Nietzsche who, with his didactic poem *Thus Spoke Zarathustra* (1883–5), drew the religion-philosophical conclusions from the modern critique of intolerance. In this work – which he himself described as a sort of 'fifth "Gospel"'[4] – he not only summed up a movement in the European

---

[3] Jan Assmann, *Die Zauberflöte. Oper und Mysterium* (Munich: Hanser, 2005).
[4] Peter Sloterdijk, *Über die Verbesserung der guten Nachricht. Nietzsches fünftes 'Evangelium'* [On the Improvement of the Good News. Nietzsche's Fifth 'Gospel'] (Frankfurt am Main: Suhrkamp, 2001).

history of ideas that has long been referred to as the 'renaissance of Zoroaster';[5] he also provided the first pattern for a fully formulated counter-counter-religion. This marked the beginning of the era of enlightened counter-zeal best characterized as after-zeal. Its central article of faith is the overcoming of binary or dualistic schematicism, which, as described above, holds the logical premise for all monotheistically inclined zealotry. The choice of the figure of Zarathustra as the mouthpiece of a post-monotheistic culture of wisdom expresses Nietzsche's idea that the first dualist is more qualified than anyone else to present the post-dualistic position – the one who errs first has the longest time to correct himself.

This is why Nietzsche was thinking less of the Mosaic than the Zarathustrian distinction – otherwise he would have had to entitle his counter-counter-religious manifesto of emancipation *Thus Spoke Moses*. The new Zarathustra was also meant to speak for a new Moses. Using the voice of the great Persian – who was once considered a contemporary of the Jewish leader – Nietzsche conceived a culture-therapeutic programme intended to put an end to the metaphysical misuse of the numbers one and two. In a fully developed form, Nietzsche's intervention in classical metaphysics and the ideology of the one ruler would have led to a pluralistically intended critique of perspectival reason – a few chapters have survived under the title *Der Wille zur Macht*, but these are barely more than sketches. In Nietzsche's case, the logical clarification of fundamentals is accompanied by a strong psychohygienic project devoted to the erosion of the resentment that leads to metaphysics. This includes the deconstruction of the obsession with the beyond, as well

---

[5] Michael Stausberg, *Faszination Zarathustra. Zoroaster und die Europäische Religionsgeschichte der Frühen Neuzeit* [The Fascination of Zarathustra. Zoroaster and European Religious History in the Early Modern Age], 2 volumes (Berlin and New York: de Gruyter, 1998), vol. I, pp. 35–579.

as every kind of *Hinterweltler*dom, i.e. insistence on a world behind our own, whose price is the betrayal of real worldly life. The author invested his best civilization-critical energies in this project, seeking to prove the statement that the philosopher is the doctor of culture. Nietzsche's critique of resentment is based on an argument that draws on the psychological Enlightenment via the notion of affective displacement. In his diagnosis, the author sees in all forms of metaphysical-religious zealotry a crypto-suicidal urge towards a world beyond in which, understandably enough, all those who failed to cope with the facts of their earthly lives hope to be granted success. Viewed from its vital and energetic side, then, zealotry is defined as a pathological symptom. When the upward glance turns into a malign fixation on the beyond, it is nihilism that lies behind the mask of religious idealism – that is to say, the compulsion to pass devaluation on to others. The name of God is then revealed as the pretext for a desire for extermination that is transferred from the inside to the outside. In its attempt to be rid of itself, the afflicted soul also seeks to prevent the world around it from continuing to exist.

Against this background, it is necessary to make a diagnostically important distinction: it makes a great difference whether one is dealing with the conventional, mild and chronic forms of world-sickness, which are embodied in convivial people's churches and can be reconciled with the joys of longevity, even a certain secularism – as has always been evident in traditional Italian Catholicism –, or rather its acute manifestations, whose followers wish to force a final decision for the good and the otherworldly. One example of the latter would be the highly active Protestant 'Doomsday sects' in the USA and their partners in the pop-culturally inflamed areas of Islamic apocalyptic thought. In such cases, the comfortable metaphysics of remembrance becomes a draft call to the holy war. Uplifting meditation is replaced by bitter activism, and religious patience with one's own imperfections and those of others gives way to zealotry in a messianic and apocalyptic setting.

For Nietzsche, such dramatizations are no more than high-flown pretexts spawned by the morbid impatience to break with reality as soon as possible; they act to fuel the suicidal fires. The apocalyptic scripts for the last days of humanity show quite clearly how suicidal and globalicidal dynamics overlap: they constitute a theatrical development of the *secundum non datur*.[6] Once one has driven into the apocalyptic tunnel, the horizon is lost, and with it at once the feeling of sharing in an environment that can be shaped. At such high levels of estrangement, any trace of responsibility for the existing world disappears. From that point on, all that counts is the hypnosis through which the activists prepare themselves for the end in holy black. With reference to these monomythical reductions, Zarathustra's approach is as current as ever. At the beginning of the twenty-first century, a time stirred up by new religious turbulence, his warning to remain faithful to the earth and send the tellers of otherworldly fairy tales to a doctor is even more relevant than it was at the end of the nineteenth.

If one applies Nietzsche's observations to today's danger zones, however, it also becomes apparent that his diagnostic instruments, as valuable as they may be for purposes of historical analysis, only reach a small part of the total phenomena. Certainly the fury of the Christian, Jewish and Muslim apocalyptic zealots of our times conceals a religiously veiled weariness of the world and life. Just as there is an endgame schema known as 'suicide by cop' among desperate criminals, one would surely find the pattern 'suicide by antichrist' among more than a few apocalyptic warriors. The vast majority of the many millions standing in line at the entrance to the final tunnel do not show any symptoms of pre-suicidal morbidity, however, but rather those of a faux-religiously channelled

---

[6] Cf. p. 96 above.

build-up of anger. For the time being, the much-vaunted dialogue of religions can hardly exert any influence on such energies. Inter-religious dialogues would only show results if they induced each organized religion to keep its own apocalyptic house in order. Moderates will observe that their respective zealots and apocalyptic warriors are usually activists with only a brief training whose anger, resentment, ambition and search for reasons to be outraged precede actual faith. The religious code exclusively serves the textualization of a socially conditioned, existential rage that demands to be let out. Only very rarely will it be possible to restrain it through religious exhortations.

What seems to be a new religious question is in fact the return of the social question on a global biopolitical level. Neither a better religion nor the best intentions can achieve anything here – as those Europeans who recall the often messianically dressed-up political troubles of the nineteenth and early twentieth centuries should know. The tools of the moment are demographic enlightenment[7] – as a critique of both the naïve and the strategic overproduction of humans – and an updated politics of development that also exports the secrets of the production and distribution of wealth to those countries previously inaccessible as a result of poverty, resentment and the machinations of perverse elites. The monotheisms know nothing about either of these – on the contrary, they are suspected of being counterproductive on all fronts.

In such a situation it is the duty of the reasonable religions, those that have passed into their respective postzealotic phases, to seek an alliance with secular civilization and its theoretical collections in the cultural sciences. Only this alliance can provide the forces that must be established and clarified in order to neutralize the apocalyptic directors. This requires the creation of symbolic

---

[7] Heinsohn, *Söhne und Weltmacht. Terror im Aufstieg und Fall der Nationen.*

terminals that give all parties in the monotheistic campaigns a feeling of victory. Only non-losers can pass through the arrival hall of history and subsequently find a role for themselves in the synchronized world. They alone will be prepared to take responsibility for tasks that can only be managed by grand coalitions.

Globalization means that cultures civilize one another. The Day of Judgement leads into everyday work; the revelation becomes an environmental report and an assessment of the state of human rights. This brings us back to the leitmotif of these reflections, which is grounded in the ethos of general cultural science. I shall repeat it like a credo, and wish it the power to spread with tongues of fire: the path of civilization is the only one that is still open.

Index

Page numbers followed by 'n' refer to a note, – eg. 33n

Abraham 20–8, 29, 31, 33n, 83, 87
absolutism 109–10
Abu Mus'ab al Zarkawi 46
activism 157
Adam 93, 97
admission ceremonies 30, 38, 87, 101
after-life 14–15, 62, 78, 85, 114–15, 141, 156–7
Allah 36–7, 38, 84, 87, 133
alphabetization 98
apocalyse 58–9, 158–9
Aquinas, Thomas 47–8
Arendt, Hannah 87
Aristotle 85, 91, 103, 148
Assman, Jan 151–2, 153, 154
atheism 23, 35, 47–8, 136, 138–9, 154
Augustine (Aurelius Augustinus) 38, 60–3, 90n, 113, 114

Babylon 28, 130, 153
Badiou, Alain 143, 144n
Baeck, Leo 53, 54, 57, 67

being 87, 102–4, 110–11
belief 17, 26–7, 42, 58, 99, 129–30
Ben-Chorin, Schalom 57
blasphemy 48, 100, 119, 134, 143
Bloom, Harold 22, 52, 68, 119n
Brock, Bazon 103, 104
Byzantine Empire 41, 113

Camus, Albert 92
Canaanites 41, 130, 153
Celan, Paul 119
Chateaubriand, François-René de 50, 126
Christianity 34, 42, 47–8, 98–9, 105, 113–15, 151–2
  expansionism 3, 55–60, 65–6
  and Greek culture 104, 151–2
  internal schisms and counter-religion 46, 108, 153, 154, 155
  and Islam 36, 37–8, 41–3, 71, 76, 113

INDEX

Christianity (cont'd)
 and Judaism 22, 33, 40–1, 44–5, 47, 57–8
 and militancy 37–8, 58–9, 69
 and monolingualism 99, 100
 and monotheism 3, 29–35, 84, 85–6, 126–7
 persecution 55, 143
 popularity 66, 80
 and ritual 31–3, 37n, 71, 99
 state religion 55, 65, 136
 and supremacy 104, 129
 and universalism 3, 30–1, 55–69
 and violence 3, 34, 42, 55, 58, 63–5, 150
 and zealotry 2, 27n, 31, 58–9, 69, 86, 107–8, 116, 158
 see also Augustine (Aurelius Augustinus); Reformation; Roman Catholicism
civilization 18, 124–5, 132, 146, 159, 160
colour 112
Communism 2, 66–7, 76, 116, 120, 136, 139, 142–8, 150, 154
compromise 112–13, 121, 131–2
cosmotheism 154
counter-religion 39, 132, 151–5
cultural religion 12, 18, 127, 131–2, 151–2

damnation 8, 61–2, 113–15
Dante 41–2, 62, 95

Dávila, Nicolás Gómez 56
Dawkins, Richard 48
death 11, 14–15, 92
Debray, Régis 44
Delacampagne, Christian 43
depersonalization 88–9
Derrida, Jacques 2–4, 105–7
Dibelius, Martin 143
Dostoyevsky, Fyodor 82, 84

ego 90, 97, 125
Egypt and Egyptians 26, 41, 73, 74, 78, 104, 130, 151–2, 154–5
Enlightenment 48, 100
 and Christianity 35, 66, 128
 and monotheism 123–4, 126, 128, 135–6
 and zeal 96–7, 136, 153, 157
ethnocentrism 31
evolution 6, 7, 137, 139
expansionism 3, 50–81

faith 13, 17–18, 47–8, 99, 125, 136, 140, 142
 and belief 11–12, 17
 and zealotry 11–12, 35, 82, 159
falsehood 93–5
Flasch, Kurt 91
French Revolution 27, 39, 127n, 153
Freud, Sigmund 25–6, 151
Fried, Erich 101

God 9–10, 20–5, 36, 50–1, 83–4, 133–4
 Old Testament 20–8, 30, 119n

see also Allah; Trinity; Yahweh
goodness 67, 87, 88, 101
Greeks 32, 51, 102–3, 104, 117, 151–2
Grunberger, Béla 45

haste 141, 144, 146, 147
hatred 123, 127–8, 130–1, 133
Hegel, Georg 1–2, 64, 88, 90, 92, 102, 105, 130–1, 134
Heidegger, Martin 16n, 82, 89, 92, 102
hermeneutics 116, 118–20
hierarchies 15, 24–5, 116–17
high culture 127
Holy Scriptures 99–100, 118–20, 121, 141–2
human rights 66, 124, 132, 160
humanism 136, 138–9, 145, 146–8
Hume, David 12
humour, monotheistic 116, 120
hysteria 82

Idealism, German 124
idolatry/imagery 42, 96, 137, 155
Illich, Ivan 34, 50
immunity 10–12, 147
inaccessibility 9–10
inhumanity 143–6
inlibration 37, 98–9
intelligence 13–14
Islam 44, 46–8
  and Christianity 36–9, 41–3, 71, 76, 113
  and compromise 112–13, 121, 132
  as counter-religion 39, 153
  and enemies/hatred 44, 130
  expansionism 3, 37–9, 69–81
  influences 71, 76, 104
  and Judaism 35–6, 42–3, 45–6, 113
  militancy 37–9, 70–8, 105–7
  and monolingualism 98–9, 100
  and monotheism 35–9, 84, 85
  population growth 79, 80
  and ritual 37, 38, 50, 71–2, 137, 148–9
  schisms and sects 46–7, 75, 108
  and supremacy 129, 137
  and universalism 3, 37–8, 69–81
  urbanism 44, 104
  and zealotry 44, 75, 108, 116, 150, 157, 158
Israel 30, 54–5, 105–6, 130

Jacobins 27, 30, 66, 67, 116, 136
Jerusalem 2, 43, 64, 105–7
Jesus 22, 30, 37n, 67, 119n, 142
jihad 70, 72, 76, 77–8
Judaism 46–8, 51–5, 130–1, 151–2
  and Christianity 22, 33, 40–1, 44–5, 47, 57–8
  and compromise 119–20, 132

INDEX

Judaism (cont'd)
  and conflict 3, 105–7
  as counter-religion 132, 153
  and idolatry/imagery 42, 137
  and Islam 35–6, 42–3, 45–6, 47, 113
  and monolingualism 98–9, 100
  and monotheism 20–9, 83, 84
  and personal supremacism 128, 129
  and ritual 27, 32–3
  schisms and sects 47, 52, 108
  and zealotry 108, 158
judgement 8, 141, 145, 148
Judgement Day 70, 89, 123, 133, 160

Kierkegaard, Søren 82, 135
Kissinger, Henry 53
Kluge, Alexander 119

language 92, 93, 97, 99
Latin 65
law 65, 134–5, 138, 145
Lessing, Gotthold Ephraim 85, 122–3, 133
Lewis, Bernard 76
logic 89, 95, 109–11, 148

McLuhan, Marshall 67
Mann, Thomas 9–10, 20–1, 129
Marx, Karl 2, 117n, 137, 142
mass culture 123–4, 126–7, 132
mathematics 89–90

meditative religions 125, 131
memoactivity 27, 71–2, 73
messianism 3, 57, 106–7, 158
militancy 37–9, 58–9, 70–1, 76, 105–7, 132, 150
missionary work 31, 37–8, 51, 55–60, 65–6
  see also expansionism
modernity 32, 65, 66, 123, 126
Mohammed 35, 36–7, 38, 43, 70–1, 76, 98, 142
monogëism 146n
monolatry 24–5, 28, 29
monotheism 84n, 125–8, 134–7
  and Christianity 3, 29–35, 84, 85–6, 126–7
  and Enlightenment 123–4, 126, 128, 135–6
  humour 116, 120
  and Islam 35–6, 84, 85
  and Judaism 20–9, 83, 84
  and supremacism 83–5, 115–17, 134–7
  and zeal 23–4, 82–92, 96–8, 108–9, 126, 155
monovalence 92–3, 95, 101, 109–11
Mosebach, Martin 17
Moses 25–8, 29, 98, 142, 145, 151, 153, 156
movements, slow 5–6
Mühlmann, Heiner 5, 6–7, 33n
murder, mass 26, 113, 144–5

Nazism 45, 130, 144
negative theology 116, 117–18

INDEX

Nietzsche, Friedrich 82, 116–17, 155–8
nous 89, 90, 91, 92

obedience 16, 86, 87, 96, 127
objectivity 88–9, 101–3
Old Testament (Tanach) 9–10, 19n, 20–5, 33, 41, 52, 90n, 119n
onto-theology 89, 91, 93, 95, 100, 102–4, 109–11
Otto, Rudolf 8–9

Paganism 42, 44, 46, 127, 130, 131, 134, 153
para-monotheism 136–7
passivity 16–18, 110–11
Paul of Tarsus (St Paul) 29–31, 33, 38, 42, 57, 58–9, 71, 76
   letters 30–1, 33, 38, 41, 58
perfectionism 83–4, 101
persecution 28, 52, 55, 130, 143, 144
Plato 87, 95, 100, 103, 137
plurivalent thinking 116
politics 78, 131–2, 138
polytheism 42, 44, 131, 153, 154
polyvalent thinking 44, 111–12, 118, 120–1
positivism 63, 64, 101
power 28–9, 126–7
prayer 43, 71–2
predestination 6, 60–2
prophets and prophecy 6, 15, 97–100, 142
Protestantism 1, 66, 68, 132
purgatory 114–15
Puritans 30, 38, 48

Qur'an 36–7, 44, 75, 99, 121
Qutb, Sayyid 43

Ratzinger, Joseph 131n
reality 29, 131, 142, 143, 158
reason 87, 153, 155
Reformation 27n, 46, 100, 113–14, 143
revelation 15–17, 140–1, 144, 160
revolution 142, 144, 145
Rilke, Rainer Maria 110n, 117
ritual 6–7, 9, 11
   admission ceremonies 30, 38, 87, 101
   and Christianity 31–3, 37n, 71, 99
   and Islam 37, 38, 50, 71–2, 137, 148–9
   and Judaism 27, 32–3
Robespierre, Maximilien 35, 39, 134
Roman Catholicism 34, 39, 86, 105, 121, 128–9, 153, 157
   and compromise 131n, 132
   and expansionism 65–6, 81
   and state religion 65, 136
Romans 30, 51, 61, 130, 153
Rousseau, Jean-Jacques 39, 48, 59n, 73, 136, 143

Sacks, Oliver 112
Sa'id Ayyub 77–8
salvation 6, 60–2, 113–15, 128
sects 46–7, 52, 78, 107–8, 157
secularism 35, 115–16, 157
self-denial 8, 96, 134–5
self-preservation 51–5

INDEX

servitude 15, 23, 59n, 85–6, 88, 104
sovereignty 51–3
spiritualization 28–9, 135
state religion 39, 55, 65, 136
stress 6–9, 27, 32–3, 37
suicide 86, 92, 103, 157, 158
summotheistic affect 21, 23, 29, 83
supremacism 82–92, 115–16, 143
  and Christianity 104, 129
  and Islam 129, 137
  and Judaism 128, 129
  and monotheism 83–5, 115–16, 137
  noetic 89–92
  onto-theology 87–9, 91, 93, 95, 100–4, 109–11
  personal 86, 88, 99, 108–9, 127–8, 129, 137
  and zeal 86, 108–9, 132–4

Ten Commandments 33, 148
terrorism 61–2, 67, 70, 79, 128
theocentrism 81
thymós 24
tolerance 43–4, 95–6, 113, 155
totalitarianism 39, 146
transcendence 5–18
Trinity 36, 56, 68, 133
truth 12, 29, 93–5, 123, 124, 139–40, 141, 148

universalism 50–81, 106, 108, 130, 131, 135, 139, 150

  and Christianity 3, 30–1, 55–69
  and Islam 3, 37–8, 69–81

vehemence 6–7, 9
violence 3, 34, 42, 44, 55, 58, 63–5, 125, 150
  see also militancy

war 38, 51, 63–5, 77, 105, 108–9, 157
Whitehead, Alfred N. 59

Yahweh 20–5, 84, 87, 90, 133

Zarathustra 156, 158
zeal
  after-zeal 150–60
  and Christianity 2, 27n, 31, 58–9, 69, 86, 108, 116, 158
  and death 77, 86, 92, 103, 157, 158
  and Enlightenment 96–7, 136, 153, 157
  and faith 11–12, 35, 82, 159
  and humanity 138–9, 145
  and Islam 44, 71–2, 75, 108, 116, 150, 157, 158
  and Judaism 26, 58, 108, 158
  and monotheism 23–4, 82–92, 95–8, 108–9, 126, 155
  and supremacism 86, 108–9, 132–4
Zoroastrism 113, 156